Improving Interperso

IMPROVING INTERPERSONAL RELATIONS

Some Approaches to Social Skill Training

Edited by

Professor Cary L. Cooper

Department of Management Sciences,
University of Manchester Institute of Science and Technology

Wildwood House

First published in hardback 1981 by
Gower Publishing Company Limited
Reprinted 1984

This paperback edition published 1986 by
Wildwood House Limited
Gower House
Croft Road
Aldershot
Hampshire GU11 3HR
England

British Library Cataloguing in Publication Data

Improving interpersonal relations: some approaches
   to social skill training
   1. Social skills—Study and teaching
   I. Cooper, Cary L.
   302'.07   HM132

ISBN 0 7045 0521 5 Wildwood House Pbk
     0 566 02277 X Gower Hbk

Printed and bound in Great Britain by
Biddles Ltd, Guildford and King's Lynn

Contents

Foreword

Dr Ron Johnson
Director of Training
Manpower Services Commission

Training in social skills has seen various 'fashions' reach their peak. Each of these thrusts, e.g. T-groups, interaction analysis and transaction analysis, has left its mark on training practices, but the discerning specialist or manager will exercise great care in choosing the best method to deal with the learning needs of the people concerned.

We now have a good deal of experience and research results to draw upon in making such decisions, but much of the information is scattered about. Often only one approach is presented without much guidance on its strengths and weaknesses and on the learning needs for which it is particularly apt.

The text brought together by Professor Cooper should prove valuable not only to trainers and managers new to this field, but also to those who have experienced some methods and would like a clear account of alternative approaches.

It is for this reason that the Manpower Services Commission has supported the publication of this book.

Notes on contributors

Dave Barker

Dave Barker is an Assistant Director of Management Studies at Roffey Park Management College, involved in interpersonal skills training and consulting with a wide variety of British organisations. He is a Special Fields Member of the International Transactional Analysis Association and a Member of the Institute of Personnel Management. He is also the author of *TA and Training* (Gower, 1980).

Professor Cary L. Cooper

Professor Cooper is Professor of Organisational Psychology and Head of the Department of Management Sciences at the University of Manchester Institute of Science and Technology. He is currently Chairman of the Management Education and Development Division of the American Academy of Management and Chief Editor of the international quarterly psychology journal *The Journal of Occupational Behaviour*. Professor Cooper is the author of over twenty books and 150 scholarly journal articles, and is a regular contributor to *The Guardian* and *The Times* newspapers.

Damien A. Dyar

Damien Dyar was a Senior Lecturer at the Limerick Institute of Higher Education in Ireland and a Lecturer at the Roffey Park Management College. Currently he is an independent management consultant.

W. John Giles

John Giles was the Manager of the Education and Training Department of Boots Limited and the Co-operative Wholesale Society. He was Vice-President of Training for the IPM (1975-77) and is currently Chairman of BACIE and the Director of the Roffey Park Management College and Institute.

Sandra V. Langrish

Sandra Langrish is a Research Fellow in the Department of Management Sciences at the University of Manchester Institute of Science and Technology. She is currently doing work on a Training Services Division research grant on Women in Management and has carried out numerous assertiveness training programmes as part of her interest in helping to develop women in management positions.

Keri Phillips

Keri Phillips is a tutor at Roffey Park Management College, specialising in interpersonal skills development for managers and trainers. He is a Special Fields Member of the International Transactional Analysis Association. He is co-author of a book on interpersonal skills training to be published by Gower in 1982. Previously he was involved in management training and development in the Home Office.

Dr Peter B. Smith

Dr Smith is Reader in Social Psychology at Sussex University. He is the author of numerous articles on T-Groups and other forms of experiential learning. He is also the author of a number of books in this field (e.g. *Groups within Organisations, Group Processes and Personal Change*) and is one of the founders of the Group Relations Training Association.

1 Introduction

Cary L. Cooper

The purpose of this volume is to provide a snapshot of each of the main approaches to social skill training currently being used in industry and the public sector in the United Kingdom. Although information is available about each of these methods, it was felt it would be useful to bring them together in one volume, so that interested managers and personnel specialists can compare and contrast their various objectives, processes and applications, and their strengths and weaknesses as learning tools. Professional trainers are sometimes inclined to seek out a particular 'flavour of the month' approach without considering the range of possibilities in terms of their own needs. This is particularly the case for social skill training and this collection is intended as a resource volume for those seeking help in selecting training methods that may help them in improving the 'people problems' and skills in organisations.

Before we begin an examination of the various approaches to social skill training that we have selected here, it might be helpful to highlight what some of the objectives of these techniques are. These methods tend to achieve one or a combination of several goals, depending on the approach; such as improvements in:

(a) Self insight

1

(b) Diagnostic skills (individual, group and organisational)
(c) Communication skills
(d) Action skills
(e) Resolution of conflict between people
(f) Team building
(g) Organisational development.

I have chosen four approaches that attempt to achieve one or more of these objectives and which are currently being used widely throughout the country. In my view they represent the main thrusts of this work.

We start Chapter 2 with a technique which is daily growing in usage and varied application, Transactional Analysis. It is an approach to social skill development which has its roots in psychoanalytic theory and method. Its main strength lies in its diagnostic framework, which is both easy to understand and goes beyond the surface level of behaviour. TA provides a structured set of concepts which enables the individual to understand the nature of relationships not only at work but in the home and social environment as well. And more importantly, it helps one to understand the 'why' of people's behaviour, unlike T-groups which are concerned with the 'here-and-now' aspects only. It can also be applied to standard management theories, particularly those of Herzberg, McGregor, etc. And finally, TA encourages change and is based on the assumption that people can change. In addition to its strengths, TA also has several drawbacks. First it possesses its own set of jargonistic language, which can have the effect of excluding others who do not understand it, and can act as a psychological barrier to protect the individual concerned. Second, since it is not here-and-now oriented, it can distance the person from his own immediate behaviour. Third, it implicitly encourages the values of assertiveness and autonomy. Dave Barker and Keri Phillips will discuss TA in greater detail in Chapter 2.

Chapter 3 highlights the widely utilised Interaction Analysis method. This technique attempts to provide the training officer with a well-designed framework for exploring interactive behaviour in small group and organisational contexts. This approach avoids some of the alleged problems with more person-centred techniques (such as T-groups), by relying more on objective and analytical tools. The main objectives of interaction analysis are (1) to increase an individual's knowledge about his/her own social behaviour through systematic observation; (2) to expand his/her information and concepts in such a way that his/her social performance will improve and (3) to understand and adequately respond to the behaviour of others. The two main advantages of this method are that (a) it enhances an individual's diagnostic skills by direct observational training, and (b) that it does this with a minimal of psychological disruption to the individual, that is, in a low confrontation way. Its main weakness lies in the absence of action plans to help the individual deal with his enhanced self insight. In addition, this approach explores only the surface level of behaviour and may not be highlighting the 'real' nature of conflicts or behaviour. In Chapter 3 Damien Dyar and John Giles provide an excellent summary of the technique, its applications and a review of its strengths and short-comings.

In the next chapter we examine Assertiveness Training, a form of social skill training which is on the ascendant, with the growing increase in women who are taking on full time careers in all aspects of industry and the public sector. This trend is particularly acute in the management field, where women now represent something near to 40 per cent of all undergraduates in management departments and business schools.

'Assertion' can be defined as 'the action of stating positively; declaring'. Being assertive means standing up for one's own basic human rights without violating the basic human rights of others. The purpose of assertion training therefore, is to help the participant to develop assertive responses in those situations in which he/she would like to improve his/her behaviour.

As with all interpersonal skills training, there are both advantages and disadvantages. The advantages can be listed as the following:

1 Enables one to influence the environment more effectively than before.
2 Improves self-esteem and feelings of self-worth.
3 Allows one to examine the appropriateness of one's behaviour in a social context.
4 May lower anxiety level.
5 Has a theoretical base, but is behaviour-oriented and therefore practical and easily transferable from a workshop situation into everyday life experiences/situations.
6 Applies to both work and non-work areas.

3

Assertiveness training has the following drawbacks:

1 Assertion training requires rehearsal and role play to be effective and some participants may find this threatening and difficult.
2 Requires examination of aspects of one's life which while being unsatisfactory may not be comfortable to confront (especially in a group versus a 'one to one' training situation).
3 Currently there is very little UK based literature or visual aids relating to assertion training.

The final technique we will explore is T-group or Sensitivity Training, which in many ways is the 'queen-bee' of all the experiential methods. It has been used in a variety of forms for nearly forty years, although its shape and colour, like that of the chameleon, have changed to suit the needs and requirements of the time. Perhaps, its very adaptability and versatility are the primary reasons for its long survival and continued usage. Under the rubric of T-groups, we find a wide variety of approaches, such as Tavistock training groups, encounter groups, gestalt groups, etc. They all have several things in common, even though they appear to the outsider as manifestly different. First, they all tend to be *process-oriented*, that is, they are interested in understanding, and making explicit, immediate interpersonal behaviour and feelings. And second, they tend to have a *here-and-now orientation*, that is, they encourage the expression of feelings and behaviour that are taking place at the time of the group training programme. Third, they tend to be *less structured* than some of the other techniques already described. And fourth, they utilise the *small group* as the vehicle for such learning. Their main advantages are that they have the potential of meeting all of the objectives one might want to consider in using social skill training, i.e., self insight, action skills, diagnostic skills, communication skills, etc. Unfortunately, they do not always achieve what they set out to, partially because of their less structured approach, but also because of their tendency to avoid a more systematic framework for diagnosis and theory. In effect, their strength of flexibility, however, can make the understanding of behavioural events that occur in these group settings less clear. Another potential weakness of these techniques is their *risk*. Many people believe these approaches to be potentially dangerous. This is a problem which I shall explore in the last chapter. And finally, these experiential groups are criticised for requiring highly trained and skilled staff, difficulty in transferring learning, and being too time consuming. The Smith and Cooper

4

chapters look at a number of these issues.

We conclude the volume with a chapter by myself which looks at a study which attempts to evaluate these techniques. It focuses on experiential learning groups primarily, but it is the kind of research which needs to be carried out on all social skill training techniques, if we are to be able adequately to evaluate their effectiveness and potential weaknesses. It is indeed one of the strengths of the T-group approach that it has spawned a large number of evaluation studies, which have helped us to understand its dynamics and potential as a training method.

Table 1.1
An audit of interpersonal or social skill training

	Advantages	Disadvantages
Transactional analysis	Good diagnostic tool	Jargon can be protective
	Can examine and express feelings less directly than T-groups	Can distance the person from his own behaviour
	Linked to standard management theories	Implicitly values assertiveness and autonomy
	Provides a framework of personality which helps to understand the 'why' of behaviour	Too psychoanalytic
	Theory encourages change and is based on assumption that people can change	
Interaction analysis	Structured framework for understanding interactive behaviour in organisations	Only deals with surface behaviour
		Difficult to use to develop action skills

	Advantages	Disadvantages
Interaction analysis (continued)	Feedback of interpersonal behaviour at work	May improve communications but in less structured way
	Little threat to individual	
T-groups	Good at developing self insight	Weak in developing action plans
	Develops group diagnostic skills	Risky for small numbers of vulnerable trainees
	Establish norms for more open communications	Need highly skilled trainer
	Can adapt for team building	Low transfer of learning from stranger groups
		Totally unstructured T-group is too time consuming
Assertiveness training	Improves self-esteem and self-worth	Trainees may find it threatening due to role playing exercises
	Allows one to examine the appropriateness of one's behaviour in a social context	Obviously places high value on assertiveness which may not be appropriate for some
	Has a theoretical base	
	Easily transferable from training situation to work	Few UK training aids available

2 Transactional analysis

Dave Barker and Keri Phillips

Introduction

The last few years have seen the introduction of transactional analysis (TA) as an approach to training for improved interpersonal skills in organisations in the United Kingdom. The number of organisations who have used, or are using, TA is a small minority but appears to be growing. It is experienced by many people as a powerful and penetrating aid to the development of interpersonal skills, resulting in a significant growth in personal awareness as well as improved communication between people. At the same time, its application in industry has not been without criticism (Kilcourse, 1978). Indeed, like any other approach, it does have its limitations, and is not a panacea for all the 'human problems' in industry. It is, however, a very significant option for the development of people in organisations.

In origin, TA is an approach to therapy, developed in the early 1950s by Dr Eric Berne, a Canadian working in the United States. However, it is a theory of communication between people as well as of individual personality, and this duality is part of its particular usefulness in organisations. The communications aspect relates to two important interests of Berne's. First, that relationships between people are a prime focus for examining and resolving personal problems. (This echoes a view of many management training and development specialists, that the 'spaces between people' are sometimes crucial to organisational effectiveness, and it also underscores team development as an approach to organisational growth.) Secondly, that individuals can be helped to improve their relationships with others if the concepts being used by the 'professional helper' are understood and actively shared by those being helped. This led to the development of a 'catchy' language for TA as distinct from traditional psychoanalytic and psychiatric practice.

Since the mid-1950s, TA in the USA has grown to become an established choice for personal therapy and in 1965 the International Transactional Analysis Association was created. Berne became known in the UK through the popularity of one of his books (Berne, 1968) and TA crossed the Atlantic in the 1960s followed later by the establishment of a British based Institute of Transactional Analysis.

The 'theory of communications' aspect of TA, together with its appealing language are fundamental to its use for social change in general, as well as just therapy. Use in organisations started in the 1960s in the US, and in 1971 American Airlines carried out their 'TACT' (TA for Customer Treatment) programme, involving over 6,000 employees (Jongeward, 1973). It was perhaps a natural development for an airline on this side of the Atlantic (Aer Lingus) to be among the first European organisations to apply TA, and the 1970s have seen its increased use in UK industry and business.

Part I TA theory
A. Ego states

This central idea was developed by Berne from his early work on intuition, and proposes the classification of individual personality into three 'sub-personalities' or 'ego states', each with characteristic attitudes, feeling, behaviour and language. The three basic ego states are referred to as the Parent, Adult and Child conventionally portrayed as shown in Figure 2.1 (referred to as a first order functional diagram).

1 *Parent*

The Parent in us feels and behaves in the same way we perceived the feelings and behaviour of our mother, father and/or others who raised us, together with other 'authority' figures we have met in our lives (from school teachers through to our latest boss).

The Parent:

  sets limits

Conditions of Worth –

8

disciplines, judges and criticises
gives advice and guidance
protects and nurtures
keeps traditions
makes rules and regulations about how life should be (the 'do's', 'don'ts', 'always', 'nevers', 'should', 'shouldn'ts', 'musts', 'ought-to's', 'have-to's', 'can'ts', 'goods', 'bads').

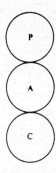

Fig. 2.1 First order functional diagram of ego states

2 Adult

The Adult is the part of us that works things out by looking at the facts, and then makes decisions. It is unemotional and is concerned with 'what fits' and what is most useful. *Adult does not mean mature.* The Adult:

gathers data from the outside world, and also from the inside, e.g. how the Child feels and what the Child wants, what the Parent says, and what the memories stored of past decisions in the Adult have to 'say'.

sorts out the best alternatives from this data and estimates probabilities.

plans the steps in the decision-making process.

3 Child

The Child in us is what and how we were as very young children with all the feelings and ways of behaving we had at that time. The Child may be:

fun loving
energetic
compliant
polite
creative
rebellious

depending on the individual.

The Parent and Child ego states are commonly subdivided into facets as follows.

4 *Facets of the Parent*

A distinction is made between the Critical Parent and the Nurturing Parent. The Critical Parent sets limits, disciplines, makes rules, keeps traditions, judges and criticises ourself and/or others. The Nurturing Parent takes care of and looks after ourself and/or others. Both have a protective role, unless over used, in which case they tend to be suppressive.

5 *Facets of the Child*

The Child ego state has two major facets, Free (or Natural) Child and the Adapted Child. The Free Child is natural, loving, spontaneous, carefree, curious, fun-loving, adventurous, trusting and joyful. The Adapted Child represents all the ways we have of getting attention from and getting along with authority figures. Our behaviour from this aspect of the Child includes not only useful things like saying 'please' and 'thank you' and 'sorry' at appropriate times, but also behaviour which can lead us into difficulties with others, such as rebellion, habitual lateness or overcompliance (always saying yes). These behaviours may have proved useful in getting others to take notice of us when we were young, but can sabotage our work and communication with others in our adulthood.

These facets of the ego states are portrayed in Figure 2.2, referred to as a second order functional diagram.

10

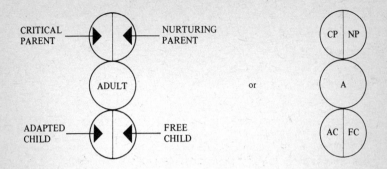

Fig. 2.2   Second order functional diagram

6   *The 'Little Professor'*

The Child ego state is sometimes considered to have a third aspect known as the 'Little Professor'. This is the intuitive and creative part of us, which understands things or people in a way that is different from the logic of the Adult. The 'Little Professor' not only has 'flashes of inspiration' but is also adept at manipulating others.

7   *Typical words, behaviours and attitudes of ego states*

Figure 2.3 gives a general idea of the characteristics of the ego states. It is important to realise, however, that this is only a guide and that the circumstances associated with the words, behaviour and attitudes are very important (e.g. tone of voice).

All three ego states are important — no one is inherently better than any other. Rather, different ego states are appropriate at different times, depending on the situation. What is helpful in relationships is to have the ability to use any one of the ego states so as to have the maximum number of choices in dealing with others.

8   *Internal dialogue*

Sometimes, the ego states interact in such a way as to absorb a great deal of energy and can cause much unhappiness. The process is referred

11

EGO STATE	TYPICAL WORDS/ PHRASES	TYPICAL BEHAVIOUR	TYPICAL ATTITUDES
CRITICAL PARENT	disgraceful ought always	furrowed brow pointed finger	condescending judgemental
NURTURING PARENT	'well done young man'	benevolent smile pat on back	caring permissive
ADULT	how? when? where? what?	relaxed attentive	open-minded interested
ADAPTED CHILD	please can I? I'll try hard	vigorous head nodding downcast eyes whiny voice	compliant defiant complaining
FREE CHILD	I want I feel great	laughing with someone uninhibited noisy crying	curious fun loving spontaneous

Fig. 2.3   Characteristics of the ego states

to as an 'internal dialogue'. For example, a manager sitting at home thinking about a work situation may have a Critical Parent — Adapted Child internal dialogue, resulting in his feeling depressed — which may be all his wife notices. The internal dialogue might be something like:

Critical Parent: 'You really dropped a clanger there; you're not meeting the standards you should!'

Adapted Child: 'Yes, what a mess I made, I'll never be able to sort it out.'

B. Exclusion

Some people exclude the use of one or two of their ego states in their relationship with other people, as shown in Figure 2.4.

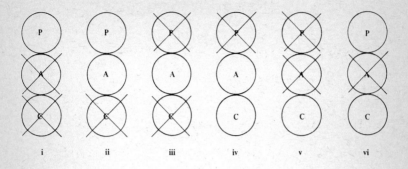

Fig. 2.4   Exclusion of ego states

If someone does have an exclusion, they are likely to be very predictable in their relationships with others. For example, someone with
an excluded Adult and Child (i) is likely to spend their time telling
everyone else what they should do (Critical Parent) and/or taking care
of others even when they don't ask for help (Nurturing Parent).
Another example is someone with an excluded Parent and Child (iii)
who is likely to be unsympathetic, unfeeling and boring.

Sometimes people have a facet of an ego state excluded. They may
have great difficulty, for example, in using their Free Child though they
might have ready access to their Adapted Child. The causes of exclusion
are related to upbringing and early childhood experiences (see following
section on Scripts).

C. Contamination

The clear thinking of the Adult is sometimes impeded by contamination. When this occurs, rational problem solving is blocked. Contamination can be thought of as an intrusion of the Parent ego state
/or the Child ego state into the Adult ego state as shown in Figure 2.5.
Contamination occurs when the Adult accepts as true some unfounded
Parent beliefs or Child distortions, and rationalises and justifies these
'truths'.

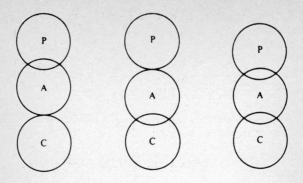

Fig. 2.5   Contamination

Parent contaminations of the Adult may show themselves as prejudices
– tenaciously held opinions which have not been examined on the basis
of current information. Grown-ups often express their prejudices to
children with such conviction that they appear to be facts. In the
context of organisations, Parent contamination in the form of prejudices acts as a considerable block to relationships between people.
For example, prejudices may cloud the way we feel about people even
before we have started to work with them, e.g. 'So you're going to do
some work with department X, are you. You'll get nowhere with them,
they're a bunch of idiots!'

A Child contamination of the Adult gives rise to distorted perceptions of reality, or illusions. For example, someone may feel as if
no one likes him and yet have no objective data as to whether or not it
is true. Yet he may believe that his feelings are the equivalent of
objective facts. In the organisation context, individuals may develop
illusions, when under stress. Also groups when devoid of information
frequently 'imagine' what's going on, and inaccurate rumours may start
to spread as a consequence.

D. Strokes

A basic concept in TA is that people want and need care, attention, love
and recognition. This is probably most clearly the case with young
children when, for example, they want to show off a new dress, have a

14

hug, or are naughty in order to get attention. Grown-ups also have ways of getting recognition by doing such things as working hard, deliberately making mistakes, coming into work late or flopping into a chair at home and saying, 'I've had a terrible day at work'. Just as people have choices about the ways they seek recognition, so there are a number of ways in which recognition can be given. This leads to the idea of strokes.

A stroke is defined as a unit of recognition. The different kinds of strokes are summarised in Figure 2.6.

STROKE	VERBAL EXAMPLE	NON-VERBAL EXAMPLE
POSITIVE FOR BEING	'I love you'	A kiss
POSITIVE FOR DOING	'Thank you for putting your toys away'	Giving an ice cream as a reward
NEGATIVE FOR BEING	'I hate you'	Child battering
NEGATIVE FOR DOING	'I get really annoyed when you arrive late for meetings'	A smack round the ear for not putting toys away

NO STROKES

Fig. 2.6 Different kinds of stroke

One key idea in TA is that negative strokes are preferable to no strokes because at least negative strokes demonstrate that 'I'm alive'. In the absence of positive strokes, many people will look for negative strokes as recognition, both in childhood (in the home) and adulthood (at work for example).

When the idea of strokes is related to organisations it seems that certain 'rules' frequently apply:

1 Don't give positive strokes freely.
2 Never give physical strokes.

3 If you give positive strokes only give conditional ones.
4 Don't miss an opportunity for giving a negative stroke.
5 Don't ask for positive strokes — certainly not directly.
6 Don't give yourself positive strokes.
7 Never refuse 'plastic' (insincere) positive strokes.

Where these rules apply then it is probable that the organisation will be a 'cold' and lonely place with very few positive strokes around. It is also likely to lead to a lot of game playing, since games are a rich source of strokes, albeit negative ones (see later section on Games).

Also, once negative strokes start to be used then they can quickly multiply and be used to score points. As a result people can spend more time arguing or 'proving' points about relationships than carrying out the tasks of the organisation. A person's personality make-up is clearly important here. For example, if somebody received a lot of negative strokes as a child — e.g. 'You're stupid! You can't think for yourself' — then when he grows up he will probably have a perception of himself as somebody who 'deserves' a lot of negative strokes and will do things (e.g. be persistently late) to sustain this self-perception. This is the idea of 'stroke balance' — individuals may seek to recreate the balance of strokes they are used to and 'comfortable' with when young (Barker, 1980). Such a person is also likely to have difficulty in accepting positive strokes and may well reject them either covertly or overtly as the following examples show.

Mr Smith: 'You did a really good job on that report, Mr Jones. Well done!'

Mr Jones: (half-heartedly) 'Oh er thanks'. (Thinks: no it really wasn't much good. I'm never much good at anything.)

Husband: 'I really like your new dress. You look very nice.'

Wife: 'No it's not really a nice dress. I look rather dowdy.'

It is therefore important for people to examine their stroking patterns, i.e. the types of strokes they give and receive and their feelings associated with them. They may be unjustly criticising themselves or others and quite possibly at the same time, denying themselves recognition of their own or others' positive qualities.

E. Life positions

The concept of life position expresses the way an individual relates to others in terms of thinking, feeling and behaving at a given time. There are four basic life positions, shown in Figure 2.7 (referred to as 'the OK corral') (Ernst, 1971).

I'M NOT OK – YOU'RE OK (I – U +)	I'M OK – YOU'RE OK (I + U +)
I'M NOT OK – YOU'RE NOT OK (I – U –)	I'M OK – YOU'RE NOT OK (I + U –)

Fig. 2.7   Life positions (the OK corral)

The following examples demonstrate the four positions:
  'Hey, we did a good job there', says the boss.
  'Yes, things are really going well for us now', says his subordinate.
(I'm OK – You're OK)
  'Your work is not up to the standard I need in this department!' says the boss.
(I'm OK – You're not OK)
  'I wish I could keep on top of things the way you do,' says the subordinate.
(I'm not OK – You're OK)
  'Well, I don't know what to do and you don't know what to do. What a mess!' says the boss.
(I'm not OK – You're not OK).
  'I'm OK – You're OK' is referred to as the 'get on with' position. People occupying this position are optimistic, confident and happy about work and life. They exchange strokes freely with those they meet and decline to put themselves or others down. Their dominant working style with others is collaboration and mutual respect, even if they disagree. Any problems they encounter they face as constructively as possible. 'I'm OK – You're not OK' is referred to as the 'get rid of' position and is characterised by feelings of anger, fury, hostility, smugness or superiority. Others are seen as inferior, unworthy, incompetent, wrong and not to be trusted. Behaviour towards others is characterised by attempts to put them down or belittle them, using criticism, spite, victimisation or abuse. At work they are likely to be highly competitive, disregarding others in their search for power and status. Whereas these people find it difficult to give positive strokes,

17

those occupyimg an 'I'm not OK — You're OK' position find it difficult to accept them. This is sometimes referred to as the 'get away from ' position, typified by feelings of sadness, inadequacy or stupidity. In this position, people experience themselves as inferior or powerless in relation to others. At work they may undervalue their skills and their potential and avoid or withdraw from difficult situations and problems. 'I'm not OK — You're not OK' is referred to as the 'get nowhere' position, and is accompanied by feelings of confusion or aimlessness and pointlessness, with a characteristic attitude to life and work of 'why bother, what's the point?'

It appears that individuals vary considerably in terms of their preferred life position, based on decisions made early in life. Some people have one position that is dominant and enduring in their relations with others, whereas other people seem to change position continually.

F. Transactions

TA is not only a theory of personality but also a theory of communication, and this duality is part of the particular power of TA. The theory of communications aspect derives from considering the 'transactions' between people using the idea of ego states. The possible types of transaction are described and illustrated as follows.

1 Complementary transaction

In a complementary transaction the individual who starts the communication sends a stimulus from one ego state explicitly to get a response from a particular ego state of the other person, and gets that response returned to their initiating ego state. Figure 2.8 gives two examples.

2 Crossed transactions

In a crossed transaction an unexpected response is returned to the initiator. The response either originates from an ego state different from that expected, or is directed to an ego state other then the one anticipated. Three examples are shown in Figure 2.9.

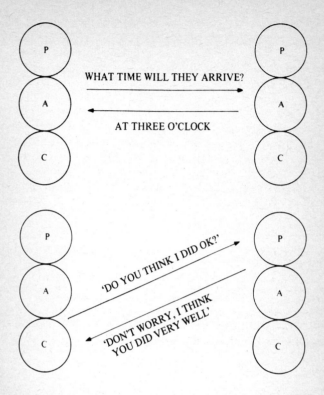

Fig. 2.8   Two examples of complementary transactions

3 Angular transactions

In an angular transaction, three ego states are involved, with an ulterior or psychological message, illustrated with a dotted line, as in Figure 2.10.

19

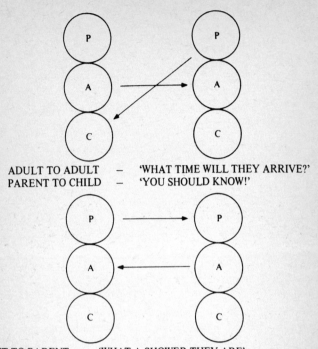

ADULT TO ADULT   –   'WHAT TIME WILL THEY ARRIVE?'
PARENT TO CHILD   –   'YOU SHOULD KNOW!'

PARENT TO PARENT   –   'WHAT A SHOWER THEY ARE'
ADULT TO ADULT   –   'WELL, I DON'T HAVE ANY DEALINGS WITH THEM'

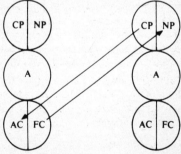

FREE CHILD TO NURTURING PARENT   –   'I WANT A NEW FILING CABINET
CRITICAL PARENT TO ADAPTED CHILD   –   'NO. WE'RE TOO BUSY TO BOTHE
                                              WITH THINGS LIKE THAT'

Fig. 2.9   Three examples of crossed transactions

20

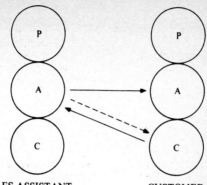

SALES ASSISTANT		**CUSTOMER**
ADULT TO ADULT (SOCIAL MESSAGE)	–	'THE SPECIAL OFFER ENDS SOON'
ADULT TO CHILD (PSYCHOLOGICAL MESSAGE)	–	'YOU'D BETTER HURRY OR YOU'LL MISS OUT'
CHILD TO ADULT	–	'I'LL BUY ONE NOW'

Fig. 2.10   An example of an angular transaction

4 *Duplex transactions*

This again involves a psychological message as well as a social one, together with the participation of four ego states, as shown in Figure 2.11.

There are no inherent 'rights and wrongs' associated with the four different kinds of transactions. Complementary transactions can proceed smoothly for long periods of time, but may signify a very stereotyped relationship, e.g. Parent – Child. Crossed transactions involve the breaking up of smooth interaction between people, and yet may be an important choice, for example, in dealing with someone who habitually uses Critical Parent. Duplex transactions can add to the richness of human contact, but in some circumstances signal the start of a transactional sequence called a 'game', with unpleasant outcomes (see next section).

21

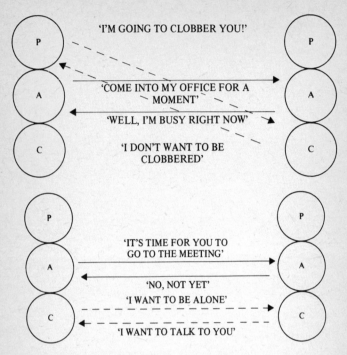

Fig. 2.11 Two examples of duplex transactions

G. Games

Games are a series of transactions involving two or more people with an outcome of 'bad' feelings (for example one person feeling inadequate and the other feeling smug). Games start with someone putting themselves or someone else down, and have a repetitive and predictable quality. They are repetitive to the extent that individuals tend to have favourite games, and predictable in that the outcomes are well defined. Games interlock: those playing 'persecutor' games (such as 'see what you've made me do') or 'rescuer' games (e.g. 'Let me do it for you' seek out 'victims' (who play, for example, 'Kick me' or 'Poor me'). The nature and intensity of games varies from person to person. In general, games inhibit effective working between people, and game analysis represents a significant way of examining and dealing with dysfunctional relationships in organisations.

22

1 Definition of a game

A game consists of a sequence of complementary and ulterior transactions which lead to a predictable outcome for both parties. The predictable outcome, or 'payoff', consists of 'bad' feelings for each player. A bad feeling is any feeling which occurs because of someone putting themselves or someone else down, e.g. anger, triumph, depression, guilt, inadequacy, etc.

Games are learned patterns of behaviour — most people play a small number of favourite games with various people in varying intensities. Game players intuitively seek out and find partners for complementary games.

2 Clues to a game

Someone is being put down.

Someone is not being straight, i.e. there's a 'hidden' or ulterior message around; alternatively something is being left unsaid. At some point the hidden or omitted information is revealed.

The people involved end up with 'bad' feelings.

Those involved may well have a sense of 'here we go again' about the situation.

3 Ways of looking at games

(a) The transactions involved

Referring to the second diagram in Figure 2.11, the transactions portrayed may well represent the start of a game. The final move may occur straight after the initial exchange shown, and the covert message revealed to give the payoff of bad feelings, e.g.

Initiator: 'You've really messed that project up.'
(payoff of righteous anger)
Responder: 'Oh, I'm sorry.'
(payoff of guilt or inadequacy)

Alternatively, the duplex transactions may continue for some time, with exchanges of pleasantries about the weather, the family, etc. before the hidden agenda is revealed. In either case, games involve a switch where the ulterior message becomes explicit.

(b) The drama triangle

This way of looking at games suggests that at the psychological level game players are aiming for, defending against, or covertly occupying a position on the drama triangle, shown in Figure 2.12. This psychological position is exposed at the end of the game.

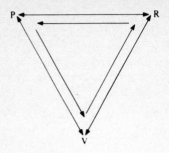

Fig. 2.12   The drama triangle

Persecutor (P): I + U − (I am better than you; you are inferior)
Rescuer (R): I + U − (I know more than you; you are inadequate)
Victim (V): I − U + (I am helpless; you are better than me)

4   *Examples of games*

Persecutor
NIGYSOB (Now I've got you, you son of a bitch. The person who typically tries to put others down and score points off them)
BLEMISH (The person who *always* finds something wrong)
CORNER (The person who verbally corners others)
LET'S YOU AND HIM FIGHT (The person who sets up arguments between others)
IF IT WEREN'T FOR YOU (The person who blames others for their own unhappy life)
SEE WHAT YOU MADE ME DO (The person who will not accept responsibility for the mistakes they make)
WHY DON'T YOU . . . YES BUT . . . (The person who can always find fault with somebody else's suggestions).

Rescuer
I'M ONLY TRYING TO HELP YOU (The person who keeps offering help − even when it is not needed − and is often upset when it is rejected)
WHAT WOULD YOU DO WITHOUT ME? (The person who likes to

24

think he is indispensable)
HAPPY TO HELP (The person who sees his sole purpose in life being to give help to others – even if they do not need it).

Victim
KICK ME (The person who contrives to put himself down)
WHY DOES THIS ALWAYS HAPPEN TO ME? (The person who feels that he is always losing out)
POOR ME (The person who feels that life is always unfair to him)
STUPID (The person who pretends that he is too stupid to understand anything)
DO ME SOMETHING (The person who always expects others to solve his problems)
HARRIED (The person who is always in a hurry and feeling harrassed).

5 *Reasons for playing games and ways of giving them up*

In the first instance, games are a powerful source of strokes, albeit negative ones. The effect for the game players involved is to make the world and the people in it appear predictable, and to help them feel that the problems they have are caused by other people. In addition, games are a way to structure time, avoiding boredom on the one hand and closeness and risk-taking on the other (see section H).

Games vary in intensity, some leading to mild upsets, some to physical damage. Avoiding games and their negative or destructive consequences may be achieved by a number of general approaches, such as:

Refuse to play the expected hand (e.g. refuse to give a suggestion or advice in a 'WHY DON'T YOU . . . . YES BUT' game).
Refuse to give or experience the expected payoff (e.g. refuse to put down a KICK ME player).
Stop inflating personal strengths or the weaknesses of others (i.e. moving into a Persecutor position).
Stop inflating personal weaknesses or the strengths of others (i.e. moving into a Victim position).
Stop taking care of others when they don't need it (i.e. moving into a Rescuer position).

Give and receive positive strokes rather than negative ones.
Structure more time with activities and intimacy (see section H).

H. Time structuring or 'what shall we do with our lives?'

One fundamental choice facing everyone is how to structure time between birth and death. There are basically six options, determined in part by the situation we are in at any given moment and partly by our own preferences.

1 *Withdrawal*

Withdrawal may be either physical (as for people in lone occupations or for those quiet moments when we withdraw to our own room or office to think, meditate or read) or psychological. It can be prompted by one of the three ego states, e.g. from the Child as a response to threat of pain or conflict, or from the Adult as a planning step.

Psychological withdrawal occurs when an individual finds little to stimulate him/her in the ongoing events (e.g. discussion, gossip, lecture) and frequently withdraws into memories and fantasies. They may be either pleasurable and creative or fearful and destructive. Withdrawal into fantasy is probably the best thing to do if the events around are dull and boring. On the other hand withdrawal may be dysfunctional if it is happening all the time, e.g. to avoid any contact with people.

2 *Rituals*

A ritual is a socially programmed use of time where everybody 'agrees' to do the same thing. It is safe, and there is no commitment to or involvement with another person. Thus in the simple, ritualistic greeting 'Good morning. How are you?', the initiator is usually not truly interested in the welfare of the other in any caring way. He is rather setting up a situation to gain a basic maintenance stroke (e.g. 'I'm fine. How are you?') by giving one in the first place.

The outcome of rituals is nearly always predictable and satisfying to the extent that we are 'in step'. As well as greetings rituals there are organisational rituals, training rituals, party rituals and so on, and they are all helpful in getting people together, without their having to get close. If the ritual and its predictability is broken, e.g. the acquaintance who has said 'Good morning' to you for the past ten years decides not to do so one day, the maintenance stroke may be replaced by a bad feeling (e.g. hurt, indignation).

3 *Pastimes*

Pastimes are transactions whereby people pass time with one another by talking about non-threatening subjects, e.g. the weather, sport, cars, shopping, bringing up children, holidays, etc. These superficial exchanges are often used between people who don't know each other well, and again result in getting maintenance strokes. Engaging effectively and at will in pastimes is an attribute of the socially competent. Some people have difficulty 'pastiming' and consequently problems in relating to others, while some do nothing but 'pastime', so don't get close to others. For the socially competent, pastimes are a form of social probing where individuals seek out information on one another in a non-threatening way prior to forming closer friendships.

4 *Activities*

Activities involve spending time in something practical and oriented towards external goals, e.g. writing a report, cleaning the car, programming a computer, building a house, shovelling snow or washing the dishes. Activities, to the extent that they are productive or creative, may be highly satisfying in and of themselves, cr they may be satisfying because of strokes received for a job well done. Doing activities may give opportunities for rituals, pastimes, games and even intimacy. However, many people use activity to avoid closeness, working nights at the office instead of coming home, devoting their lives to making a million instead of making friends. Activities may also be a rich source of negative strokes, e.g. doing a dull and boring job.

5 *Games*

Games are referred to in the previous section. They may only occupy a short time in a person's day, but still be very significant in their consequences.

6 *Intimacy*

Intimacy is a state characterised by:

spontaneity
honesty, trust, candidness
shared feelings, thoughts and experiences
heightened awareness
no ulterior transactions, no games
access to all three ego states.

It is essentially a function of the Free Child, and seems to be innately present in infants until or unless parental influences interfere. It is unpredictable and unprogrammed and can be risky and frightening, with the potential for personal rejection.

Intimacy occurs not only in the context of sexual, emotional, aesthetic, recreational and spiritual expression, but also in such areas pertinent to organisations as:

work and the sharing of common tasks
commitment and joint investment in common goals
conflict, where there is a mutual concern and effect to resolve difficulties and problems
creativity and thought, where there is joint involvement in the development of new ideas.

In conclusion, games are nearly always destructive whereas withdrawal, pastime, rituals and activity are only dysfunctional when they are a predominant form of time structuring. Indeed withdrawal can be relaxing and restorative (lying on the beach reading, meditating), pastimes fun, and rituals even more so (bonfire night, Christmas), and activities full of self-expression (activity is not destructive unless the compulsion to keep busy is one and the same as the compulsion to keep apart). Many people experience little intimacy in their lives and yet it is the richest source of positive strokes.

I. Stamps

Stamps, or to give them their full title, trading stamps, are feelings that an individual collects and stores, rather than expresses at the instant they were experienced, and then discharges at a later date. As an example consider the following story. Bill Smith was Production Manager at the Symbiosis Drug Company. His job was challenging, stimulating and tough. On Monday, one of his foremen was late for the fourth time in a month, and volunteered a trivial excuse. Bill said nothing. On Tuesday, the quality control department checked the same batch twice by mistake. Bill said nothing. On Wednesday someone damaged a fork lift truck and on Thursday one of the suppliers sent the wrong material. On Friday his secretary missed a sentence from a memo to the Managing Director, and Bill finally lost his temper. His unfortunate secretary bore the brunt of it. During the week Bill had been saving anger stamps, and on the last day he cashed them in with a great outburst.

Psychological trading stamps are so called because of certain parallels to the commercial variety.

They are collected and stored till some future date (Monday to Friday for Bill Smith).

Different individuals collect different types. Some people collect bad feelings (brown stamps) and some people good feelings (gold stamps). The bad feelings collected may be even more specific, e.g. anger (red stamps, as for Bill Smith) or depression (blue stamps), guilt, hurt, etc.

Eventually the stamps are redeemed. Different people collect different quantities and have different compulsions as to when, where and how they redeem them. Some cash them in for a small 'prize', e.g. throwing a rubber at the wall, losing temper with some- one else over a small mistake, taking a day off. Others cash them in for a big 'prize' such as taking company property (brown stamps), firing an employee (brown stamps) or taking a week's holiday (gold stamps). Sometimes the 'prize' can be really big, for example losing the company a lot of money, getting fired, having a breakdown or even suicide. In all cases this cashing in or redemption time is accom- panied by a sense of justification, which is often indicated by the phrases a person uses, e.g. 'I couldn't stand it any more'; 'That's the last straw' (said Bill Smith); 'Given all that's happened, what else was there to do?'

Some people review their stamps extensively, e.g. go over all their hurts and angers before going to sleep at night, while others 'put them away in drawer' and forget about them for weeks, months or even years. Sometimes people review their collections with one another and by this means pick up 'secondary stamps' on behalf of others, e.g. 'Is that what he said to you? Of all the nerve, that makes me really angry.'

Stamp collecting is a serious hindrance to effective working relation- ships. For example the boss who collects anger stamps and cashes them in for a free rave at his subordinates once a month may well have problems of commitment from his team. His other choice of course is not to collect the anger stamp in the first place, but rather to talk openly with his subordinates at (or as near as possible to) the time of their mistake, transgression or poor performance. As another example, an employee may tolerate appalling treatment from his boss for years without a murmur, and then one day go in and wreck a piece of machinery, when all his pent up feelings explode. Again there is another choice, that is to express his feelings and needs by directly confronting the 'put downs' as they occur and, in more extreme cases, change his job.

J. Rackets

The chairman called his executive directors together for an important board meeting prior to the publication of the half-yearly reports. 'Well gentlemen', he said smiling, 'we've had a good six months and my congratulations to you all for your support and effort.' All but one of his fellow directors relaxed and smiled with him. 'However, good though the results are, they're not good enough', he said slowly and grimly. 'I must call on you and your staff to put more effort in during the next six months!'

> The managing director felt confused.
> The sales and marketing director felt inadequate.
> The production director felt guilty.
> The research and development director felt miserable.
> The administration director felt scared.
> The financial director felt angry and started to think which one of his colleagues to blame.
> The wise old personnel director noticed each of his colleagues getting into their racket feelings . . . and kept his own counsel.

In this little story, all but one of the directors were 'caught' by the chairman and ended up in their 'racket' or 'racket feeling', i.e. the bad feeling payoff at the end of a game. Many people seem to have one particular racket and consequently it is sometimes referred to as their '*favourite* bad feeling'. For example, some individuals have anger, while others have depression, confusion, hurt, fear, or inadequacy. Any feeling may be a racket feeling. Some people seem to have more than one racket feeling, whereas a few don't seem to have one at all.

Racket feelings are Adapted Child substitutes for spontaneous Free Child feelings which in some way were not 'permitted' in childhood. Both are instantaneous and both are really felt. However, there are some important differences as shown in Figure 2.13.

Rackets are considered as being learnt under the influence of one or more of the following processes:

   1 Straight modelling for a child by a parent, i.e. a racket is passed on by example. For example, a son sees that his father has a tendency

Racket feelings	Real (reactive) feelings
Arise from Adapted Child	Arise from Free Child
Learned, substitute way of getting strokes.	Spontaneous, without concern for consequences.
Often experienced by others as manipulative and false. This is particularly the case when the feeling is apparently incongruent with the rest of the person's behaviour.	Usually experienced by others as authentic since the feelings expressed are appropriate in type, intensity and duration.
Repetitive, with no useful action taken by the individual. Indeed the racket feeling may be used to block problem-solving behaviour.	Once expressed are done with and the individual moves on to fresh business.

Fig. 2.13: Racket feelings and real feelings

to get angry almost regardless of the circumstances.
2 By stroking into a child's behaviour. For example a daughter learns that the only way to get attention from her mother is to look sad and depressed.
3 By telling a child what to feel or think. For example, an angry child is told . . . 'You're tired and need to go to bed'. This can lead to a tiredness racket, if it is consistently repeated.

K. Scripts

One of the most powerful ideas in Transactional Analysis is the concept of Life Script, first elaborated by Berne (1975). A Life Script is a personal plan decided on at an early age (4-7 years old) by each individual in response to external events. The most important external factor for an offspring is the behaviour, attitudes and influences of parents, or, in their absence, other authority figures. On the basis of this influence, we make decisions about what kind of person we are and what kind of life we are going to lead, these decisions being crucial to our well-being and 'survival' when we are young. The problem is that the decisions or adaptations we make at this time may be disruptive in our relationships with others when we are older. The powerful effect of parental messages is based on the situational constraints facing children. For example they are very small when compared to parents, are often not given much information about what is going on, or are given distorted information. Last of all they have no choice to leave and find a better place to live!

The basic idea in scripts, therefore, is that frequently, because of childhood decisions, people mould their lives according to a self-fulfilling prophecy. The raw material for the development of scripts depends on the 'permissions' and 'injunctions' which are prevalent in the child's home. For example, the child may be encouraged (permission) to think for himself, but discouraged (injunction) from expressing affection. These permissions and injunctions may be expressed directly or indirectly. That is, the child might be told, 'Don't trust people or show you care for them because they'll take advantage of you', or he may see his own father keeping his distance. In the light of this the child might well decide that in order to be accepted by his father (and avoid negative strokes) he must think for himself and not get close to people. This childhood decision may be carried into adulthood and circumstances where it is not longer useful. The person may grow up to be independent and self sufficient, but have great difficulty in establishing close relationships. In other words, a script of loneliness has been established and will be supported by the kinds of transactions, games, time structuring and stamp collecting the individual participates in.

For healthy personal development of the child the following permissions are likely to be of considerable importance:

To exist, to be accepted, loved and welcomed into the world.
To express feelings.
To think and to develop his problem-solving abilities.
To be close and express affection for others.
To be the sex he/she is.
To be the age he is, and not to be encouraged to stay a child or grow up before his time.

Without these permissions a dysfunctional script may develop and be passed on from generation to generation.

Organisations, particularly small family concerns, are sometimes re-garded as having scripts. There may be permissions and injunctions prevalent in an organisation which leads its members, for example, to feel that they must do everything in a hurry, or never have any fun or never express feelings. The relationship between individual and organi-sation scripts has yet to be fully explored, but it seems possible that people may work in organisations which have a script matching their own.

Part II TA as a training aid

A. The main concepts of TA

As a basis for looking at TA as a training aid, Figure 2.14 shows the main concepts of TA in relationship to one another.

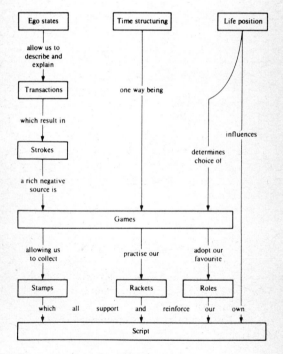

Fig. 2.14   The main concepts of TA

33

B. The aims of TA

1 *In TA terms*

Taking each of the main theory areas of transactional analysis discussed in this chapter in turn, the aims of TA are:

Ego states
Reduce dysfunctional Parent and Adapted Child behaviour. Develop the ability to choose behaviour freely from each of the three ego states as appropriate.
Increase access to Free Child creativity.
Reduce/remove contaminations.

Strokes
Increase exchange of authentic, positive strokes and decrease inauthentic positive strokes and negative strokes.

Life positions
Increase the time spent in I+ U+ position as opposed to the other three life positions.

Transactions
Increase the awareness of the consequences of different kinds of transactions in interpersonal communication.

Games
Reduce the extent of games.
Avoid taking positions on the drama triangle.

Time structuring
Spend more time in intimacy.
Increase or reduce the time spent in activities as appropriate.
Increase skills in pastiming (in certain situations).

Stamps
Reduce stamp collecting and replace with more effective management of feelings.

Rackets
Replace racket feelings with reactive feelings.

Scripts
Reassess personal destiny and, where appropriate, make new decisions.

Two important things need to be said here. First, some of these goals may not be achievable through training, but are rather the domain of therapy. Much depends on the individual concerned and the severity of the issue. Second, most of the goals are phrased in terms of reduction (or increase); it is questionable whether 'destructive' behaviour can

34

always be eradicated by an individual, with or without help from others. For example, conditions of severe personal stress for someone sometimes lead to a return to the 'bad old ways'.

2 *In training terms*

In general terms, TA can be used to aid the following training and development goals in organisations:

Improve relationships between people, so that there is less misunderstanding and fruitless 'fighting', and better communication.

Decrease manipulation, put downs and 'executive politics', and increase straight open honest authentic interaction.

Increase understanding about 'what goes on' between people.

Help people grow, develop and increase their sense of self-confidence and self-responsibility.

Reduce self-defeating behaviours.

Increase people's ability to assert, i.e. state their wants in a direct way and get their needs met, as opposed to being aggressive and hostile, devious and manipulative, or withdrawing and avoiding.

C. Areas of application in organisations

The most potent use of TA is in interpersonal communications both within an organisation and with the contacts and customers of an organisation. In the latter case it can help advisers and consultants examine their client relationships, help in training staff in selling skills and aid those involved in ongoing contact with the public. It has potential value in recruitment interviewing and in industrial and commercial negotiation.

Within an organisation, TA gives a new way of looking at management and leadership style (e.g. with the use of such concepts as contamination and exclusion), can contribute to the development of appraisal and counselling skills (e.g. with use of the drama triangle concept), and help develop the creativity, problem-solving and decision-making skills of groups. Many practitioners see the most valuable use of TA to be in team building, i.e. the development of the interpersonal skills and goal planning abilities of a section or department of staff (e.g. stroke exercises can be used as a basis to give and receive feedback in teams. Apart from team building, TA has a general contribution to make to Organisational Development (OD) in that many of its concepts can be used at a 'macro' level to look at the style of an organisation. TA has also been used to examine the origins and nature of the mid-life crisis (Novey, 1976).

Finally, there are some more diverse areas for the application of TA in organisations. These include the training of trainers in group handling skills (many games are played between trainers and trainees), a new approach to the old problem of effective time management (using time structuring), a possible explanation of some forms of accident proneness (using strokes and games), and as an aid to the development of influencing and assertion skills for women in management and for racial minority groups in organisations (Jongeward, 1973).

Within these areas of application TA has a great deal of versatility and can be used in a variety of ways as Figure 2.15 demonstrates.

AIMS	METHOD	TIME
1a Encourage people to think about themselves and their relationships. 1b Give a flavour of what TA is and what it can do	Mixture of TA theory (ego states, strokes and transactions) and reinforcing exercises (see Barker, 1980).	½-1 day
2 Help trainees develop interviewing and counselling skills.	Mixture of TA theory (ego states, transactions, strokes and games) and role plays using TA as an observation and feedback tool.	2-3 days
3 Help trainees develop group leadership and membership skills	Mixture of TA theory (ego states, transactions, strokes and games) and role plays using TA as an observation and feedback tool.	2-3 days
4 Team building (i.e. helping a group of people from the same organisation to work together more effectively).	TA theory together with exercises which encourage the giving and receiving of feedback 'positive ping-pong', (e.g. see Barker, 1980). Role plays could be used as an intermediate step between the theory and feedback.	4-5 days
5 Personal awareness and personal growth training (i.e. encouraging people to explore themselves and their relationships in the 'here and now').	The leader can use TA as the basis of interventions in the group, e.g. 'You seem to have a rule about . . .' (Parent), 'What do you like about yourself/others?' (Strokes)	4-5 days

Fig. 2.15   Versatility of input of TA

D. The use and consequences of TA in the US and the UK

This section refers briefly to the application of TA in the United States (Jongeward, 1973, Carby, 1976), and the United Kingdom and mentions the authors' experience with using it.

In the United States the approach has been used in a number of organisations, including the Bank of America (Manager – Subordinate relations), Bell Systems (Sales Training) and American Airlines (Customer Contact Skills). Some limited evaluation of the Bank of America work has been made. The programme involved four one-day sessions, usually one week apart, involving 15 to 30 managers. The aims included providing an approach for developing relationships between people, increasing awareness of the importance of personality as an influence on communication and acquiring new choices for behaviour. Methods included the use of questionnaires, exercises, group discussions, a film, personal diaries, and personal feedback. The theory covered included scripts (briefly), life positions, strokes, time structuring, ego states, transactions and games. A sample of 68 participants, going back up to three years, responded to a questionnaire. The majority reported that they (1) were more effective in handling those who were either overly dependent or highly authoritarian, (2) found the learning useful both at home and at work, and (3) found it helped them with the toughest problem they were facing at the time they were involved in the programme.

Whilst there are the usual problems of drawing firm conclusions from this kind of feedback, the results do indicate some of the benefits and payoffs of TA.

In the British study (Carby, 1976) feedback of programme outcomes was of an individual and anecdotal nature, with no reports of adverse effects and several mentions of other benefits outside work. The programmes concerned varied from half to four days and were mounted to deal with such needs as managing changed employee expectations, improving customer relations and resolving problems of group performance and behaviour. The same publication quotes the use of TA as a component of a major OD programme to produce a more 'people sensitive' organisation, with several spinoffs including the extension of TA training, team building, job redesign programmes and the changing of some corporate 'sacred cows'.

In the authors' work at Roffey Park (Barker, 1980) TA is used in a variety of training situations involving the development of personal awareness, interpersonal skills and group effectiveness. More specifically TA is used as a tool in teambuilding programmes, counselling courses, advising skills workshops and interviewing training. Whilst the feedback on the Roffey Park work is again individual and anecdotal, it appears that TA leads to more satisfactory and effective relationships, and to greater self responsibility and determination.

One major step that is now required is a thorough evaluation of the consequences of TA training for a specific group or organisation, perhaps along the lines of Cooper's and Bowles' work (1977).

E. Disadvantages of TA

1 TA has a jargon which can be off-putting and misleading. Where a group is being exposed to TA for the first time it may be worth the trainer's while keeping the jargon to a minimum (e.g. saying 'aspects of personality' rather than ego states) and to be sure of using examples which will be of immediate relevance to the course.

2 TA can potentially provide material for manipulating others, e.g. putting people down by calling them 'niggysobbers', or establishing boundaries between those who have been 'initiated' in TA and those who have not. There is no obvious and easy way of avoiding this problem, but clearly the trainer has an obligation to confront these sorts of behaviour when he sees them. (In any case, the evidence is that other approaches to interpersonal skill training also have this problem.) If the trainer engages in this kind of behaviour himself then he will reduce his own effectiveness and devalue TA. It is important for any trainer using TA to look after his or her own training and development through appropriate courses and workshops, and in this way to be sensitive, for example, to any favourite games he might have.

3 TA is a potent model that can go deeply quite quickly. For example, it is possible that simply on the basis of some theory (especially scripts) trainees could feel unsettled and uncomfortable about their relationships. They could, for instance, start reflecting on how they treat their children. It is important for the trainer to be alert to the reactions of the trainees, and to stress that people can change. It may also be worth considering some small group work where people will probably be more willing to express any fears, doubts or concerns which they might have.

4 TA implicitly values autonony (i.e. people being responsible for themselves and their feelings) and assertiveness (i.e. people being

direct about their wants and needs). If autonomy and assertiveness are not valued by the organisation then the trainee may find it difficult to fit in after training and equally, his boss may find him more 'difficult' to manage. It is important therefore for the trainer to do what he can to check out the expectations of the trainee's organisation (Kilcourse, 1978).

5 TA was originally developed as a novel approach to therapy and only later developed into a more broadly applicable tool for education, development and training. Some people react negatively to it because of its origins in therapy, and certainly it is important that trainers themselves are clear about the boundary between their work and that of therapists. For example it is highly inappropriate for a trainer to invite a course member actually to re-experience themselves as a six year old (referred to as 'regressive work').

F. Advantages of TA

1 As discussed previously, one of the major strengths of TA is its versatility. It can be used simply as a theory, or as the basis of helping people to develop interpersonal skills (1:1 within groups and between groups) or as a means of encouraging people to examine and express their feelings about themselves and others. Also, depending on the needs of the group and the objectives of the training, the emphasis can be readily adjusted. For example, if the theory is readily accepted by the group then the trainer can make an on-the-spot decision to go more 'deeply' by introducing some exercises.

2 TA can also be used as the underlying theme of basic management courses which look at such topics as motivation, delegation, interviewing and problem-solving. TA can be related to some "standard" management theories and ideas: Maslow's Hierarchy of Needs, McGregor's Theory X and Y, Herzberg's Motivation-Hygiene Theory, Likert's four types of Management systems, Blake's Managerial Grid, etc. It appears that none of them is dissonant with TA theory and indeed can be positively integrated with it.

3 The theory provides an integrated view of personality (ego states), communication (strokes and transactions) and destiny (scripts). The trainer and the trainees therefore have the opportunity, if they want it, to go beyond a person's behaviour and look at the motivation for it. Information on the 'why' can be important in helping people to change. The theory also provides an integrated model of thinking, feeling and

doing, three basic human characteristics.

4 The theory is usually readily accepted and is seen to be applicable to a wide range of circumstances both at work and in non-work situations. It also gives people a common language for analysing behaviour.

5 TA clearly identifies the options which people have in the ways in which they relate to others. The trainer can always say as part of a feedback and review session, 'What other ego states could you have used? What do you think the consequences would have been?'. TA also values experimentation rather than right answers. It therefore implicity encourages people to try things out and decide what makes sense for them.

6 There is an important and optimistic value in TA that people can change. This is of crucial importance in training where, if the possibilities of change are denied, then the value of the training is severely reduced.

References

Barker, D. M., *TA and training: The Theory and Use of Transactional Analysis in Organisations*, Gower Press, 1980.

Berne, E., '*Games People Play: The Psychology of Human Relationships*', Grove Press Inc, 1969; Penguin Books, 1968.

Berne, E., '*What do you say after you say Hello? – The Psychology of Human Destiny*', Grove Press Inc, 1972; Corgi, 1975.

Carby, K., and Thakur, M., 'TA at Work', Institute of Personnel Management, 1976.

Cooper, C. L., and Bowles, D., '*Hurt or helped*', Training Information Paper no. 10, Training Services Agency, 1977.

Ernst, F. H., 'The OK Corral: The grid for getting-on with', *Transactional Analysis Journal*, vol. 1, no. 4, 1971.

Jongeward, D. et. al., *Everybody Wins: TA Applied to Organisations*, Addison-Wesley, 1973.

Karpman, S., 'Fairy tales and script drama analysis', *Transactional Analysis Bulletin*, vol. 7, no. 26, 1968.

Kilcourse, T. A., 'TA under attack', *Personnel Management*, June, 1978.

Novey, T. B., '*TA for Management*', Jalmar Press Inc, 1976.

3 Interaction analysis

Damien A. Dyar and W. John Giles

Analysing interactive behaviour

Interactive situations at work

Interaction is the basis of the task group – the 'meeting' which features so frequently in organisations. Interaction is also the basis of the social group – the non-task activity which again is common to work organisations. Equally important in terms of interactive skill is the 'semi-focused' task group. This is the situation where a group of colleagues loosely discuss areas of concern within their organisational setting. They may not appear to be doing so in a directed manner, no firm decisions may be made, but their discussions will affect the general flow of decisions within the firm. We are not concerned only with the 'meeting'; the interview, whether it is about selection, appraisal, problem-solving, or talking to a customer, is also based on interaction. Thus in any work situation where people come together, either in a direct task context, an incidental task context, or as a social group, interaction and the skills of interaction become important.

What happens in these situations? What is the essence of interaction? Fundamentally, people communicate with each other. They talk, either about the task or non-task matters. As students of interaction, there-

41

fore, we want to know what is said. Better still, we want to know how it is said — what true meaning lies behind the words used. We also want to know who said it and to whom, when it was said, and where it occurred. In addition to talking, messages will be conveyed non-verbally, whether by gaze or gesture, so we will want to observe the pattern of non-verbal behaviour and interpret its meaning. Between the area of verbal and non-verbal behaviour a kind of semi-talk may occur and this, too, can be rich in meaning. Into this category we place grunts, groans, and mumbles (grumbles?). A highly sophisticated approach to inter-action analysis would give a fine reading on all of these areas, but we may have to settle for less because of the nature of behavioural science research tools. The remainder of this section is devoted to presenting some of the methods available for the analysis of interaction and to pointing up some research findings associated with these methods. Each is presented in a simple form, and uses, advantages and drawbacks are outlined.

Common to most of the situations with which we are concerned is the need for a smooth and motivationally satisfying interaction to take place. Participants need to establish a certain minimum level of *rapport* with others in a meeting or interview. They should be motivated to continue the interaction towards task goals within a pattern which is socially comfortable. Members will also need to display sufficient sensitivity to the stresses and anxieties within the interaction to enable them to maintain equilibrium by reducing anxiety or releasing tension. In short they will need to exercise such social techniques as are necessary to maintain the interaction. This need provides a common thread through many different interactive contexts. We can view it as a basic element of interactive skill and as such it might provide a starting point for interaction analysis. Argyle (1969; 1972) gives some clues as to how a smooth and motivationally satisfying interaction might be encouraged. He suggests that synchronisation between inter-actors is necessary along the following dimensions:

1 Amount of speech	This should take up most of the time of inter-action, allowing for natural pauses. Overtalk and interruption should be kept to a minimum.
2 Speed or tempo of interaction (pace)	The rate of words per minute, the length of pause before replying, and the rate of body movements, contribute to the pace of inter-

	action. If the interactors differ widely on these, dissatisfaction, irritation or stress may result.
3 Dominance	May be treated in terms of contributions and/or in terms of relationship. Where there is agreement between both on who is dominant there is less likelihood of conflict.
4 Intimacy	Can be seen as a function of physical closeness, eye contact, intimacy of topic, etc. Here again, difference between the interactors' behaviour or perception of how they ought to behave may lead to one viewing the other as cold, stand-offish, intrusive, or over-familiar. Where difference occurs, adjustment may involve high motivation costs to one or both participants.
5 Competition and co-operation	Both parties must agree on the competitive or co-operative elements in the interaction.
6 Emotional tone	Incompatible reactions or remarks lead to dissonance and lack of equilibrium.
7 Task, topic and procedure	It sometimes occurs that interactors have different perceptions of the job they are doing, the topic they are discussing or the procedures they ought to adopt. Efficient task performance and smooth interaction require a measure of agreement on these items.

These factors might be seen as common to many interactive situations and awareness of them may help an analysis of what is occurring in general terms, but if we wish to have a deeper understanding of what is happening we can progress to measuring details of behaviour. Some approaches to such measurement are presented in the next sub-section.

Measuring behaviour

1 *Interaction flow*

This asks who speaks to whom. Two measures may be used:

(i)   each comment by an individual may be counted ('scored' is the term we shall use);

43

(ii)   the time spent in talking may be registered.

From this we can derive the percentage of interaction allotted to each individual and the direction of comment. Advantages of this approach are that it enables us to measure who is dominating or who is not contributing; who are high, medium and low contributors. The main drawbacks of this system are that used by itself the content and meaning may be missed, and it is also difficult to register non-verbal behaviour. The interaction flow may be presented as a matrix (Figure 3.1) or in diagrammatic form (Figure 3.2); both figures illustrate the same data.

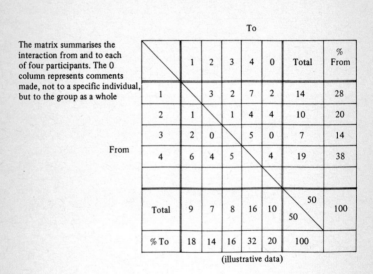

The matrix summarises the interaction from and to each of four participants. The 0 column represents comments made, not to a specific individual, but to the group as a whole

	To						
	1	2	3	4	0	Total	% From
1		3	2	7	2	14	28
2	1		1	4	4	10	20
3	2	0		5	0	7	14
4	6	4	5		4	19	38
Total	9	7	8	16	10	50 50	100
% To	18	14	16	32	20	100	

From

(illustrative data)

Fig. 3.1   Interaction flow matrix

The diagrammatic representation shows in a dramatic way the flow of exchanges and the focus on each member. Each line represents a transmission from a member to another or to the group as a whole and arrows give direction. Lines going outward from the group indicate comments directed to the group as a whole, e.g. Person 1 made two comments to the group.

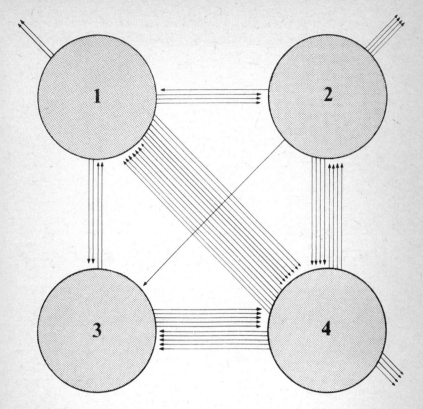

Fig. 3.2   Interaction flow diagram

2 *Role analysis*

It is possible to analyse roles adopted by interactors. This may be done
by asking participants or observers for their perception of the role performed by individuals. For example, frequently it is desirable to analyse
leadership in a group. We may identify this role in advance and ask
observers to note instances which demonstrated where leadership lay
in the group. We can go on to ask them to describe the functions performed by the role incumbent. To illustrate:

Michael: I think we should move on to the next topic. John, would
you bring us up to date on stock figures . . . I trust they will be (er)

more precise than last time.

Frank: Before you do that, John, I would like to thank you for getting those production schedules to me yesterday . . . they were very useful indeed.

Even in this short exchange there is evidence that different roles are being taken. Michael displays behaviour which suggests he is leading the group, e.g. moving the topic on, selecting the next item, calling on John to contribute. There is also an element of censure ('more precise than last time') which might suggest a leadership link to previous meetings. Taken by itself, Frank's comment may be deemed irrelevant to the task in hand, but in the light of the censure in the previous contribution it may be seen as supportive towards John. We could go on from here to assess how frequently Frank has provided a supportive role in the interaction or Michael a leader role; thus some quantification is possible within role analysis.

There may be a number of roles which are identifiable in advance, or during the course of interaction, such as initiator, agitator, scapegoat, developer, co-ordinator, and so on.

This type of analysis gives a qualitative assesement of role perception and function and, if coupled with some more quantitative measure of interaction, can be a useful tool. The main disadvantages are the highly subjective nature of the perception and the fact that content of inter- action (e.g. contributions to the task solution), may be missed by selectively looking at major roles.

3 Content analysis

Instead of 'who spoke to whom' analysis as in interaction flow, we might further ask 'who said what to whom?' The 'what' element is immense! In any interaction a wide range of different things may be said by any one individual. It is necessary therefore to reduce these somehow to a manageable size. The answer to this problem has been to categorise behaviours in advance and then place contributions into one of these categories. The use of behaviour categories is gaining in popularity and a number of different approaches will be presented below.

It is usual for observers to mark each contribution by an individual into an appropriate category and at the end of the interaction to total how many contributions each individual has in each category. From there the percentage of contributions in each category can be derived.

The approach in general is useful for getting at the content of interaction: 'what is said'. Some of the systems also provide for scroing of non-verbal behaviour. The complexity of certain approaches makes them difficult to use in the training situation, but beyond this the advantages and weaknesses are specific to the scheme and the situation in which it is being used.

The systems below are currently being used in training situations. They are not the only ones: they have been selected to illustrate some approaches without necessarily implying that there is an ideal method.

Interaction process analysis. This is perhaps the most widely-used system for analysing interaction. Devised by Bales (1950) over thirty years ago, it seeks to relate categories of behaviour to their problem areas. This scheme helps to identify phases in problem-solving.

Groups working on a 'fully-fledged' problem will show a phase movement: 'the process tended to move qualitatively from a *relative* emphasis on attempts to solve problems of *orientation* (what is it) to attempts to solve problems of *evaluation* (how we feel about it) and subsequently to attempts to solve problems of *control* (what shall we do about it)' (Bales, 1953).

Behaviour in each phase is classified as either questioning behaviour, such as seeking orientation, or answering behaviour, such as giving an evaluation. The orientation phase is characterised by giving or asking for information, clarification or confirmation, or by repeating or asking for repetition. The evaluation phase is characterised by giving or asking for opinions, feelings or wishes, or by other behaviours which attempt to evaluate the topic or points made. The control phase is characterised by seeking and giving suggestions. Giving a suggestion is indicating a potential method of problem solution, e. g. 'perhaps we should pay an incentive bonus for this job'. Others have autonomy in that they may reject the suggestion.

Bales uses categories which relate to problems of orientation, evaluation and control, and he distinguishes between questions and answers. Figure 3.3 demonstrates these categories, which together represent the *task*-related dimension of interaction.

A second dimension which Bales uses incorporates behaviours which are of a *social* nature, e.g. supporting a group member of lower status than others, or are of an *emotional* nature, e.g. demonstrating tension. This dimension is called the *social-emotional* dimension. Behaviours are classified as social-emotional *positive*, such as agreeing, supportive or tension-releasing activities, or alternatively they are classified as social-emotional *negative*, such as disagreeing, showing tension, or showing

47

Category	Behaviour Illustration	Phase or problem area	
Answers			
Gives suggestion	Direction, solutions, implying autonomy for others	Control	*Questions*
Gives opinion	Evaluating, analysing, expressing wishes or feelings	Evaluation	
Gives orientation	Informing, repeating, clarifying, confirming	Orientation	
Questions			
Asks for orientation	Seeks information or clarification, seeks confirmation or repetition	Orientation	*Answers*
Asks for opinion	Seeks evaluation, analysis, asks for expression of feelings	Evaluation	
Asks for suggestions	Seeks direction, solutions	Control	

Adapted from R. F. Bales (1953)

Fig. 3.3   Interaction process analysis: task dimension

antagonism.

Figure 3.4 demonstrates the *social-emotional* dimension. The problem area associated with agreeing, or disagreeing, in decision-making. Demonstrating tension, or tension release, is related to the

Category	Behaviour illustration	Problem area	
Positive:			
Shows solidarity	Raising other's status, helping rewarding	Integration	*Positive*
Shows tension release	Joking, laughing, showing satisfaction	Tension management	
Agrees	Agreeing, passively accepting, understanding	Decisions	
Negative:			
Disagrees	Disagreeing, showing passive rejection, withholding help	Decisions	*Negative*
Shows tension	Withdrawing, seeking help	Tension management	
Shows antagonism	Deflating other's status, defending or asserting self	Integration	

Adapted from R. F. Bales (1953)

Fig. 3.4   Interaction process analysis: social-emotional dimension

problem area of tension management. Showing solidarity, or antagonism, is expressive of the extent of integration between inter-actors.

Analysis of typical actions and reactions recorded by interaction process analysis shows that about half of the acts during a group problem-solving session fall into the giving of information, opinion, or suggestion, a further fifth fall into agreeing/disagreeing, with the remaining categories having a fairly even distribution. This is necessarily the 'best' pattern but there is evidence to show that groups expressing satisfaction demonstrate more suggestion-giving, more information-giving and more agreeing than groups expressing dissatisfaction. The latter demonstrate more opinion-giving, more asking for orientation, more asking for suggestions and more disagreeing behaviour (Bales, 1953). It was mentioned earlier that problem-solving groups have been found to move through phases of *orientation, evaluation* and *control*. In the first phase groups are collecting information, then weighing it according to task, group, or personal criteria, and finally group members are pressing toward a decision with a 'concomitant increase in support for some members and a rejection of others' (Hare, 1962). Social-emotional behaviour increases during each of these phases, but positive reactions increase more rapidly in the final phase. It has been suggested by Hare (1962) that the *decision point* is critical; once it is passed, the rate of negative reactions diminishes and the rate of positive reactions increases. As the task is settled by the decision the group then turns to its social-emotional needs.

Groups who meet repeatedly over time tend to demonstrate a rather different social-emotional pattern. Early positive social-emotional behaviour tends to be centred on showing agreement. This may subsequently decrease and be replaced by a rise in behaviour directed to showing solidarity and tension release. Thus there is a shift from task-related agreeing behaviour to the more emotionally positive solidarity and tension release behaviour as meetings progress. Bales (1953) identified an *'equilibrium problem'* in that groups characteristically oscillate between behaviour directed to task solution and behaviour directed to group maintenance and the satisfaction of the needs of members. They swing from task absorption and neglect of individuals' needs to concentrating on group solidarity and neglect of the task. This problem of maintaining equilibrium between task and social-emotional behaviour is one of the many factors related to group productivity.

The nature and duration of phases in group activity may differ

49

according to the nature of the activity and the influence of situation factors like the degree of consensus between members about their relative status.

The Bales system has been used effectively with problem-solving groups. It is a complicated system, however, and in its original form may be unsuitable for many training purposes. Later we will suggest an alternative form of interaction process analysis for use where time or limited capacity to assimilate may inhibit usage of the full system.

A further difficulty in using interaction process analysis has been identified by Klein (1963). The categories appear tidier than they are. It can be extremely difficult, for example, to distinguish some remarks which might be either opinion or suggestion.

Klein's interaction schedule. The schedule has borrowed heavily from Bales' work and is expressed in Figure 3.5. Klein's view is that task-related behaviour has a factual aspect and a value aspect. Facts are categorised under the heading of *giving or asking* for *information*. She argues that facts are impersonal. They cannot be altered by discussion.

Dimension	Category	Notation	
Task-related factual	asks for information	inf	−
	gives information	inf	+
Task-related combining facts and values	asks for views	vi	−
	gives views	vi	+
	makes explicit proposal (optional category)	pro	
	disagrees	agr	−
	agrees	agr	+
Task-irrelevant, expressive, evaluative only	expresses hostility	expr	− h
	expresses withdrawal	expr	− w
	expresses friendliness	expr	+ f

From Klein (1963)

Fig. 3.5   Klein's interaction schedule

Values on the other hand are not verifiable. They are personal and express an individual's judgement of the value of an idea or express his preference for a particular course of action. The schedule does not attempt to provide for a dimension which categorises values by themselves but suggests that in social situations people express ideas which are a combination of values and facts. 'Views' is the term which might

50

categorise this: ' "views" are sentences in which facts and values are presented in a ready made combination' (Klein, 1963). Views are sometimes expressed as *explicit proposals*, which she suggests may be used as a separate category. Agreement or disagreement complete the combined task-related dimension.

An illustration of these categories is given in the following exchange:

Speaker	Contribution	Category
Member A:	Let me make it quite clear. My party will not accept this policy	Information +
	We feel that the underprivileged members of the community are not getting a fair share	Views +
Member B:	Seventy-five per cent of revenue is going to alleviating the cost of sickness to old people!	Information +
Member C:	I propose that this item be put back to the Council's next meeting	Proposal
	Would that be the best course?	Views −
Member A:	Nonsense! We've got to reach a decision now	Agrees −

The remaining dimension is expressive of feelings which are irrelevant to the task. It has positive and negative elements. Expressions of *withdrawal* which refer to the flight, dissociation or retreat of a group member are seen as negative. Other negative behaviours are categorised under the heading of *hostility* towards the task or other members of the group. Positive behaviours are categorised as expressing *friendliness*.

Categories in this interaction schedule are probably easier to score than in the Bales form of interaction process analysis. The distinction between facts and values is a useful addition. As with the Bales system, the dramatic break between task and non-task behaviour may be more apparent than real and it is possible to miss behaviour where there is both a task element and an affective or social-emotional element (Hare, 1962). The introduction of positive and negative evaluations in the task area is potentially misleading as negative might imply that the behaviour hinders achievement of task goals and this may not be correct.

The two systems of behaviour classification presented so far have generally been described in relation to problem-solving groups. General

51

systems can be too broad-based to suit specific types of interaction; recent attempts at classification have tended to develop systems which are more narrowly focused. One interesting example is a system of classification focusing on interaction in negotiating groups – conference process analysis.

Conference process analysis. Stephenson and Morley (1970) suggest that observation of negotiating groups will require recognition of a number of dimensions. The central dimension is *resources* which are exchanged between each party. A second dimension is the *mode* by which resources are exchanged – 'offered', 'sought', 'accepted', 'rejected', 'yielded', or 'withheld'. The third *referent* indicates to whom the behaviour refers. The scheme also allows for use of a *time* dimension – when the events occurred and whether or not the act is a direct response to an act initiated by some other person. A number of other behaviours can also be categorised within the system and these are outlined in Figure 3.6.

Procedure	covers the way in which the conference is conducted.
Outcome	refers to all proposals which set a limit on the final agreement.
Threat	contains all reference to conditional statement of hostile intent.
Acknowledgement	recognition or praising the contribution of a party or participants.
Provocation	provocative or derogatory statements.
Description	other facts and opinions expressed.

Fig. 3.6   Conference process analysis

Conference process analysis is still being developed, but it has been presented here because it provides a useful approach to the dimensions of interaction in negotiation. It introduces the concept of resources being exchanged, which is a central theme in negotiation. The scheme is complex in that it appears to require handling at two levels simultaneously (i.e. the 'dimensions' level and the 'behaviour' level). The key dimension, 'resources', can be elusive and requires very sensitive interpretation.

At the inter-group level Douglas (1962) has identified a three-stage development for negotiating groups. This differs from Bales' in that the first stage, *establishing the bargaining range*, is characterised by an exhaustive and thorough probing of the outer limits of the range within which they will negotiate. At this point the parties emphasise the differences between them and project the 'impossibility' of reconciling the disparities. Speeches are long, and formalised, and antagonism is displayed. Such antagonism is, however, between the parties rather than between individuals on either side. The second stage, *reconnoitring the bargaining range*, is characterised by a move from the more formal and public behaviour of the first state to individual and interpersonal activity. These informal activities may include private 'chats' between individual members of both parties. They do not commit the parties, but they open the bargaining so that room for movement can be explored. The third stage, *precipitating a decision-making crisis*, moves activities back to the more formal level where offers are made between groups as they strive to reconcile the conflict between them. Douglas suggests that this phase sequence characterises successful negotiation.

In another study of negotiating groups Landsberger (1955) demonstrates that a phase sequence equivalent to that suggested by Bales correlates with successful negotiations. This point is taken up by Stephenson (1971), who suggests that there may be consistency between the findings of Douglas and Landsberger in so far as: the 'orientation' phase is equated with 'establishing the bargaining range', the 'evaluation' phase is comparable to 'reconnoitring the bargaining range', and 'control' is not dissimilar to 'precipitating a decision-making crisis'. Stephenson points out, however, that the phase movement is less clear for 'social-emotional' behaviour, particularly in relation to 'antagonism' in the early stages. It is possible that unless negotiators are sufficiently mature to understand the 'impersonal' nature of early hostility their negotiations will be less successful.

Behaviour analysis. Another model has been developed recently by Rackham et al. (1971). Originally developed for social skill training of supervisors within the air transport industry, more recent applications have been made in a wide range of occupational settings. Several different sets of behaviour categories have been suggested by the authors to meet the needs of specific interactive situations. One set of categories is presented here under the title of behaviour analysis, which the authors have adopted: see Figure 3.7.

These categories have the advantage of being more readily understood than some of the other schemes presented. The information provided by the analysis has been used to reconstitute training groups according to the behaviour profile shown.

In this section we have presented various approaches to content analysis. One content area has been given scant treatment thus far: nonverbal behaviour. It is possible to score certain non-verbal behaviours in categories such as 'shows tension', but it has become obvious in recent

53

Category	Description
Proposing	A behaviour which puts forward a new concept, suggestion or course of action (and is actionable)
Building	A behaviour which extends or develops a proposal which has been made by another (and is actionable)
Supporting	A behaviour which involves a conscious or direct declaration of support or agreement with another person or his concepts
Disagreeing	A behaviour which involves a conscious or direct declaration of difference of opinion or criticism of another's concepts
Defending/Attacking	A behaviour which attacks another person or defensively strengthens an individual's own position. Attacking behaviour usually involves overt value judgements and often contains emotional overtones
Blocking/ Difficulty stating	A behaviour which places a block or difficulty in the path of a proposal or concept without offering any alternative proposal and without offering a reasoned statement of disagreement. Blocking/ difficulty stating behaviour therefore tends to be rather bald, e.g., 'It won't work' or 'we couldn't possibly accept that'
Open	A behaviour which exposes the individual who makes it to risk of ridicule or loss of status. This behaviour may be considered as the opposite of defending/attacking, including within this category admissions of mistakes or inadequacies proving that these are made in a non-defensive manner
Testing understanding	A behaviour which seeks to establish whether or not an earlier contribution has been understood
Summarising	A behaviour which summarises, or restates in compact form, the content of previous discussions or considerations
Seeking information	A behaviour which seeks facts, opinions or clarification from another individual or individuals
Giving information	A behaviour which offers facts, opinions or clarification, etc.
Shutting out	A behaviour which excludes, or attempts to exclude another member
Bringing in	A direct and positive attempt to involve another

Based on Rackham (1971)

Fig. 3.7   Behaviour analysis categories

years that non-verbal behaviour is a significant input and feedback factor in social interaction and the following section is devoted to it.

4 *Analysis of non-verbal behaviours*

Non-verbal cues are important to the understanding of what goes on in interaction. What are we looking for? Argyle (1969) has suggested that the non-verbal elements of social behaviour may be grouped under the following headings:

(a) Body contact. This varies enormously from one culture to another. Main types of contact: hitting/aggressing, caressing/stroking, greeting/farewell contacts, guiding another's movement.

(b) Proximity and positioning. Distance at which people stand or sit apart from each other may give clues to the degree of intimacy between them or alternatively to the nature of the topic or situation. Proximity varies with different situation. Individuals' positioning may change (e.g. as they get closer together they move from face-to-face positioning to side-by-side).

(c) Posture. This may reflect attitude to the group (e.g. slumping and inattentive), status (informal/formal), or emotion.

(d) Physical appearance. This is usually fairly constant during interaction, but may change as interactors relax, e.g. taking off one's coat.

(e) Facial and gestural movements. Facial expression may demonstrate emotion; provide a continuous feedback; act as an attitude indicator; modify or comment on what is being said or done. Hand movement may illustrate what is being said; replace speech by gesture; show emotional state (e.g. nervous fiddling); be concerned with self-grooming.

(f) Gaze direction. This is one of the most important aspects of non-verbal interaction. Gaze may be used to establish a general or a specific kind of relationship (e.g. 'intimate' gaze). It may reflect the need for feedback about the meaning of the interaction (e.g. a questioning look). It may be used as a control device between participants.

Finally we may also wish to register non-verbal elements of speech, e.g. an encouraging grunt, or the emotional tone of speech.

It is worth repeating that the primary reason for looking at behaviour in the training situation is to improve skill in relation to organisational objectives. Observing behaviour in isolation may be fruitless; therefore the analysis should note the behaviours *in terms of their influence on group objectives*. The behaviour should be related to the context in which it occurs, and in the next section we consider some of the situations on which the trainer may wish to focus.

Use of interaction analysis for improving skills

How can interaction analysis be used to improve skills in working with people? In this section we will illustrate some uses of the systems for analysing interaction that have been presented. Our objective is to help training personnel develop interaction analysis as part of their own programmes in the development of human resources. A brief initial review of training methods will help to place subsequent comments in perspective.

Training methods

By far the most common method of learning work-related social skills is by observing colleagues doing the job. Satisfactory methods for on-the-job training in social skills have yet to be devised, though many of the ideas developed in off-the-job training should be applicable in the actual work situation for continued learning. One goal then of off-the-job training should be to enable social skill learning to continue in the post-training situation.

Off-the-job training methods are currently considered to be the optimal approach to social skills training. Groups are placed into situations for analysis by the introduction of role-playing or by using the group behaviour as a medium for analysis. This latter method is frequently adopted by 'T-group' and other types of 'sensitivity' training, and is covered in Chapter 5.

Our illustrations in this chapter will therefore mainly refer to the role-playing approach. Role-playing is frequently augmented by instruction or discussion of concepts relevant to interactive skills.

The training group is a primary resource: members are selected to 'play' roles which equate to the situation for which skills are being developed. One member may play the role of interviewer while another (or alternatively a pre-briefed 'external' helper) acts as interviewee. Or one half of the group may role-play a management meeting while the other half observe and take notes on the interaction.

The learning principles behind such role-playing are that trainees: (a) get an opportunity to practise interaction skills; (b) improve their insight into and understanding of the interaction process; (c) develop self-awareness and self-perceptions. The process of adaptation and improvement of skill in social interaction is thus encouraged.

Success, however, may depend on what the trainer does or helps trainees to do with the knowledge and experience gained. First the links

56

between the role-playing situation and the trainee's work situation need to be made. This may be helped by seeking work-related problems in advance and using these as a basis for role-play. It may also be helped by the use of roles with which the trainee is familiar or by 'role-reversal' where, for example, a shop steward may be asked to play the role of the industrial relations manager. The most important mechanism for making links to the practical situation is appropriate feedback. This aspect is developed below.

A second difficulty encountered with the use of role-playing is interpretation of 'what is expected' by trainees. They may over-dramatise the situation, or treat it as an occasion for an entertaining 'send-up', or in some way play to the audience of observers. Careful briefing and orientation usually help to overcome these problems. It is also helpful if trainees are impressed with the need to 'be themselves', as far as is possible in a somewhat artificial situation. An understanding of the concepts behind the training programme may also help to in-crease commitment.

Because of the drama and novelty that exists in role-playing there is a danger that the role-play becomes the primary activity of the training group. There is little point, in terms of improving interactive skills, in role-play without careful analysis and feedback. The analysis/feedback process is essential for skill improvement. Opinions vary on when feed-back should take place. Most writers on interaction training are agreed that it should take place as soon as possible after the action occurs, but there are difficulties associated with giving feedback. One approach is for the trainer to interject with his evaluation of a particular behaviour, or to interject with a question which directs the attention of the group to the behaviour, thereby bringing about feedback from other group members.

Rackham (1971) suggests that this type of feedback requires a highly qualified (and highly expensive) trainer, which might be too costly for many organisations. He also suggests that too much intervention gives rise to the problem of identity between trainer and group: he may be-come too closely integrated with the group. On the other hand, a very large number of behaviours are generated by a group and too much delay is likely to lead the trainer (and the participants) to forget much of what has gone on. In order to overcome these difficulties, Rackham used a 'qualitative data based' approach in the training programmes developed in BOAC. Here five-day courses were divided into three stages:

1 A diagnostic stage: during the first three days, intervention by trainers was kept to a minimum while behaviour of the group in a variety of interactive situations was categorised.

2 A formal feedback stage: on day three, group and individual feedback on behaviour pattern and performance was given by trainers. This was backed by quantitative data gleaned during the first three days.

3 A practice and monitoring feedback stage: on the remaining two days, participants were encouraged to 'experiment with different behaviour patterns and to monitor their performance by examining their behaviour analysis results periodically'.

We have devised training courses where participants provide a major feedback role. This approach introduces group members to the interaction analysis method in the early stages of training, i.e. after a brief conceptual foundation has been laid. Participants are subsequently given an opportunity to test the uses of the interaction analysis method on a 'demonstration' or pre-taped video recording (an audio tape recording would suffice). Subsequent role-playing activities divide the group into observers and interactors, so that all members get several opportunities to be both role-player and observer. After each role-play the observers report using whichever aspect of the analysis method they have been asked to concentrate on as a framework. The analysis, feedback and discussion are led by the trainer, who uses a video-tape recording of the interaction to illustrate points of effective or non-effective social performance.

So the feedback may either be given by the trainer, backed by quantitative data and observers'/interactors' impressions; or it may be given by the observers, backed by quantitative data and the trainers' impressions; and the course can be designed so that feedback occurs fairly soon after the interaction, or it may be felt desirable to withhold feedback in the early stages of a course while behaviour patterns are building up. There is a lack of comparative research in this area and course designers may feel the need to try a number of alternatives. Such evidence as there is, however, does support the view that both oral and recorded feedback help the process of skill acquisition (Argyle, 1969; Rackham, 1971).

The point should be made here that quantification of interaction as a basis for feedback tends to characterise training programmes which assume the skill-based approach. The sensitivity-based programme (or in the terms we used earlier, the 'social-based course) depends rather more on group introspection. The process of interaction analysis is represented in Figure 3.8.

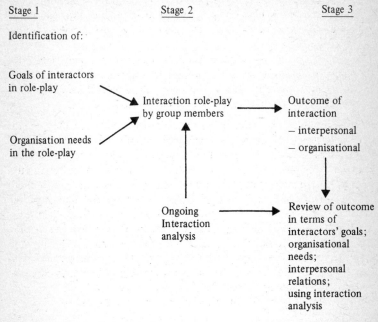

Fig. 3.8   Interaction analysis

Evaluation

Two broad approaches to evaluation of this form of training may be distinguished: (i) evaluation of adaptive learning taking place during the training experience; (ii) on-the-job type evaluations by self or others of perceived improvement in skill areas. We may:

(a) measure change/improvement in observed behaviour during the course of the training;
(b) ask trainees to assess their colleagues' skill improvement during the training experience;
(c) ask trainees to rate changes they feel have happened to themselves;

(d) rely on trainers' perceptions of skill improvement;
(e) ask co-workers, subordinates, or superiors if they perceive changes in the individual's behaviour after the training.

Ultimately, on-the-job evaluation is the most important in terms of organisational needs and requirements. If training courses in the area of interactive skills are mounted after careful analysis of individual and organisational needs, the ongoing evaluation of behaviour (and behaviour change) during training can be made more meaningful. This enables objectives to be set within the context of organisational needs and thus a formal *validation* of the training can be carried out based on these objectives.

The selection of appropriate criteria is important. What sort of behaviour is it necessary to improve, and what needs to be avoided? Criteria should be selected according to the training objectives and not on a basis of value judgements about what is 'good' or what is 'bad' social behaviour. For example, there is little point in demonstrating that an individual's 'building' behaviour has increased as a result of training if this behaviour is not important to the job situation.

It is important also to evaluate the *reliability* of the method of interaction analysis being used in the training. *Reliability* of the method means the extent to which different observers rate interactions similarly or the extent to which the chosen system regularly picks up items of interaction that need to be known.

Readers who are interested in pursuing the question of valuation may be interested in the practical approach to evaluation developed by Warr et al. (1970). This approach suggests a framework for evaluation which they have dubbed CIRO. CIRO stands for the initial letters of context, input, reaction and outcome evaluations. They suggest that evaluation may embrace: (1) Context evaluation – determining training needs and objectives from information about the current operational context; (2) Input evaluation – choosing between alternative 'inputs' to training on the basis of information about possible training resources; (3) Reaction evaluation – information about current or subsequent reactions in order to improve training; (4) Outcome evaluation – information about the outcomes of training in order to improve subsequent training: this might be in terms of immediate, intermediate and ultimate outcomes.

Evidence of the effectiveness of interaction analysis is growing, but there is as yet little guidance on which approach is best to meet specific objectives. Research shows that social skill can be improved by repetition, but that the amount and quality of improvement is related to the availability of feedback. On-the-job training would provide wide scope for skill development through repetition, provided an effective coach were present to give feedback to the trainee. Argyle (1969) has summarised this evidence: he concludes that specific skills, e.g. interviewing, are enhanced by the use of role-playing techniques and that discrimination and interpretation of interpersonal cues can be improved. The evaluation process can be used as an important aid to the quality and nature of the feedback given to trainees as well as a monitor on the effectiveness of the whole training programme.

Context of interaction

In this section we will look at some of the different situations in which skill is needed, under three headings: (a) two-person interaction; (b) group interacting; (c) inter-group interaction.

(a) *Two person interaction*

We have avoided the term 'interview' in the sub-heading as this conjures up for many the image of the 'selection interview'. In fact, organisational life throws up a series of two-person interactions which follow an activity pattern that might be described as 'interviews'.

Apart from the obvious 'selection interview', many will be conscious of 'appraisal interviewing' or 'counselling interviewing'. Some other types of interviews are problem-solving, discipline, briefing, exit, customer or grievance-focused activities. The amount of two-person interaction in organisations will vary, but one study has shown that managers speed on average a third of their work hours in two-person interaction (Stewart, 1967). The range varied from 23 per cent of managers' time in the lowest of the samples to 39 per cent in the highest.

As an illustration of using interaction analysis within two-person situations we have, however, chosen the selection interview. Fitting a suitable candidate for an existing job within the organisation is the underlying purpose of the interview. The main objective of the interviewer is to make the right decision. Our focus will be on how far his skill as an interviewer contributes to the making of a good decision.

The trainer must give the trainees some criteria against which the decision can be evaluated. Use might be made of a selection plan which incorporates a system of job analysis, e.g. the scheme devised by the National Institute of Industrial Psychology (NIIP, 1972). From this, goals or objectives of the interview can be delineated. Thus it will be possible in the interaction analysis to relate the interview to goals and organisational requirements.

A similar concern with the relationship between interaction and the context within which it occurs should exist in the case of meetings or groups interacting.

From the schemes identified in the previous section we will illustrate here by drawing from the interaction process analysis system of recording, as applied to the selection situation. The full recording system developed by Bales (1950) may be too complex for short training activities. The authors and their colleagues at the Roffey Park Institute have used a modified version of the system for management training in interviewing skills. This version retains the distinction between contributions which are primarily task focused and contributions which are primarily social-emotional focused. A recording form such as that represented in Figure 3.9 may be used. Here the interviewers' and interviewee's contributions are scored separately and sub-totalled. The percentage of each category within the total interaction may now be

Category	(a) Interviewer		(b) Interviewee		Category Total	
	Score	% of total (a)+(b)	Score	% of total (a)+(b)	Score	% of total (a)+(b)
Social-Emotional POSITIVE	8	5.3	4	2.7	12	8.0
Social-Emotional NEGATIVE	2	1.3	8	5.3	10	6.6
Social-Emotional TOTAL	10	6.6	12	8.0	22	14.6
TASK QUESTIONS						
Asks for suggestions	8	5.3	0	0.0	8	5.3
Asks for opinion	9	6.0	3	2.0	12	8.0
Asksfor information	15	10.0	12	8.0	27	18.0
Task Questions TOTAL	32	21.3	15	10.0	47	31.3
TASK ANSWERS						
Gives suggestion	14	9.4	15	10.0	29	19.4
Gives opinion	11	7.4	17	11.3	28	18.7
Gives information	6	4.0	18	12.0	24	16.0
Task Answers TOTAL	31	20.8	50	33.3	81	54.1
TOTAL	73	48.7	77	51.3	150	100.0

(Illustrative data)

Fig. 3.9   Interview interaction analysis

derived. This information enables us to compare the nature and direction of task behaviour and the type of social-emotional behaviour.

Taken by itself it can be a useful tool for analysis, but there are gaps which need to be filled. The first point has already been made: we need to fit this record to its context. Is this task pattern one which fitted best the objective of our selection interview? This can only be answered with a full knowledge of the selection situation, but a casual glance at our illustrative data would immediately raise questions as to the nature of the suggesting and opinion-giving by the interviewer. Is this the sort of pattern we would expect from a selection interview? The analysis cannot give us the answer. We need to know in detail the situation, and fortunately we can also supplement the interaction analysis with other forms of observation.

The data in Figure 3.9 give us a breakdown of major qualitative areas, but too much concentration on the resultant quantities may lead to a misdirected interpretation. We might supplement it with direct observation of the questions asked by the interviewer, e.g. are they presented in an understandable manner; are they open or closed; are they leading; are they reflecting something just said; are they building on what is happening; are they probing more deeply; are they flexible or do they follow a rigidly predetermined sequence? The quantitative knowledge we already have will be supplemented by illustration of these aspects. Each trainer will decide which points need to be emphasised. Of course, he may want to add other areas of his own to meet the needs of his situation. In a similar manner it may be desirable to have more than a head count of social-emotional contributions. Some of the areas previously outlined as contributing to smooth interaction are not picked up at all, or only indirectly, so they too may need analysis.

(b) *Group interaction: problem-solving and decision-making*

Groups in organisations have a wide variety of functions. Among the most common are decision-making, problem-solving, consultation or briefing groups.

There are many common areas of analysis between interviewing and interaction at group level. A familiar work-group activity is the problem-solving meeting. We are concerned not only with the abilities of the group members to communicate with each other, but also with their effectiveness as a problem-solving group. We must, therefore, observe the activities of the group in relation to its decision-making processes.

Of great interest to students of problem-solving groups, are the 'phases' of group activity. For example, earlier we mentioned Bales' (1950) concept of groups moving through 'orientation', 'evaluation', and 'control' phases. The concept may be a useful starting point for observation but we will also need to look at other elements. The section of this chapter on research delineates some factors which distinguish one group from another, e.g. access to resources, power, cohesion of members, specialisation of role, etc.

Analysis should, therefore, include consideration of the manner in which structural variables such as these enhance or inhibit task effectiveness. These may be observed both as input factors and as factors which develop during the course of the interaction. For illustrative purposes we will refer to Klein's (1963) scheme and its usefulness for analysing interaction within a meeting.

From whom	To whom	Task related							Expressive f h w	Content reminder
		inf +	inf −	vi +	vi −	(pro)	agr +	agr −		

After Klein (1963)

Fig. 3.10   Klein's interaction schedule

The analysis method suggested by Klein is presented in Figure 3.10. This form can be extremely useful where the trainer has to carry out the analysis. As each contribution is recorded serially, the final result is a 'blow' by blow' account of the interaction. It can also give an accurate picture of interaction flow through the summation of the first two columns. It enables this purely quantitative measure to be related to the qualitative categories outlined. These are: information ±; views ±; (proposals); agrees ±; friendliness; hostility; withdrawal. Two useful suggestions have been added by Klein: that a note of the content will help observers to recall the behaviour; and that instead of

64

just ticking the 'agrees' categories the recording observer might distinguish between implied and open agreement or disagreement by marking 'i' and 'o'.

It might be desirable to supplement the interaction schedule with more descriptive questionnaires. What, for example, of role specialisation? Who performed the 'leader' role? Was it possible to isolate various 'leader' roles such as task leader and 'expressive' (or social-emotional) leader? What specialist contributions were important to the problem-solving — how were these drawn out? Who acted as facilitator or as thought-provoker? How effectively was the role of chairman performed in drawing information and views together and helping to integrate them into concrete proposals; in securing agreement and commitment? How might the chairman's style be described? Was it most appropriate to the context and the participants?

We might also look at the effectiveness of group performance. Was it worth getting together; could individuals acting alone have come to a more useful decision; who inhibited or enhanced performance? Were effective procedures adopted to facilitate group activity? How adaptive were rules or procedures?

Again the 'culture' of the group could be assessed. Was there a co-operative or competitive orientation? Was there high dependency on certain members; who were they and why? Was there 'pairing', coalition, or clique-forming? How cohesive or integrated was the group? The meeting, as with the interview, will have the common elements of social interaction previously described. It may be desirable to analyse these, e.g. amount of speech, dominance, intimacy, emotional tone, non-verbal cues, etc.

The problem-solving group in work situations is not a single homogeneous type of group. Therefore we can look at interaction differences between groups with different structural or personality mixtures. Committees which have an informal ethos and lack of clearly defined hierarchical status (e.g. some research and development meetings) may not require exactly the same social skill as formal meetings with a clearly established chairmanship. We can observe interaction patterns in both situations and compare and contrast the skills needed.

(c) *Inter-group interaction: negotiation*

The most dramatic organisational illustration of inter-group interaction is negotiation between management and unions, and we will use that as a base for illustration. But there are other situations where the inter-group focus is present, e.g. inter-departmental meetings, shopfloor/ supervisory meetings, client/sales meetings.

It may be argued that interactive processes between groups do not differ from interactive processes within one group. Thus the same approach might be taken as for the problem-solving meeting. On the other hand it can be argued that relationship and focus are more strictly defined in the inter-group situation.

The areas of difference have been pointed out in a previous publication, where it was suggested that negotiation training could be approached from a number of different perspectives (Dyar, 1973). For the purposes of illustration our analysis is confined to the local or micro-level bargaining. A system of interaction recording developed by Stephenson and Morley was introduced in the previous section. Its dimensions demonstrate the difference between negotiation and problem-solving. For ease of recording, the forms shown in Figures 3.11 and 3.12 may be used.

| By | To/from | Resources | | | | | | Context reminder |
		Offered	Sought	Accepted	Rejected	Yielded	Withheld	

Fig. 3.11   Conference process analysis, form 1

This information is presented with reference to the parties or sides in the negotiation. It may, of course, be used to observe individual contributions. It has weaknesses in that there is little scope for observing the impact of pre-negotiation influences. Supplementary analysis may start with that point. It can be an extremely useful vehicle for observing the manner in which a party's case has been represented; it allows the strategies, tactics and movements to be observed. Figure 3.11, which is concerned with the central dimension of 'resources', is constructed as

66

a serial recording of the interaction. It shows the source and direction of resources offered, sought, accepted, rejected, yielded or withheld. Figure 3.12 is used to summarise other behaviour categories on a group

Behaviour category	Party A	Party B
Procedure		
Outcome		
Threat		
Acknowledgements		
Provocation		
Description		
Totals		

Fig. 3.12   Conference process analysis, form 2

basis. The technique of 'i' (implied) and 'o' (open) recording may also be useful, i.e., an offer of resources may be implied rather than openly declared. However, in the training context it may be necessary to utilise further measures of behaviour. Rackham (1972) has devised a scheme which the authors have found usefully complements conference process analysis in negotiation training situations. This utilises categories of proposing; building; supporting; disagreeing; defending/attacking; blocking/difficulty stating; testing understanding; summarising; seeking information; giving information; open. There is of course some overlap between the two which needs to be rationalised, especially the similarity between threat/provocation and defence/attack.

Rackham's method of dealing with the minutiae of interaction is to slow the whole operation down by isolating the two groups from each other and then passing written communications between groups. The procedure he outlines is that each participant of one group writes down what he would say in the face-to-face situation. The group then selects one member's contributions to send to the other party, where in turn each member writes down his response. The second group then selects one of these responses to send back to the first, where the procedure begins again. This is time-consuming: building up a fairly mean-

67

ingful sequence of interaction may take a morning. It is therefore more suited to courses of several days' duration. It is a useful method of observing the growth of conflict between groups.

References

Argyle, M., *Social Interaction*, Methuen, London 1969.
Argyle, M., *The Psychology of Interpersonal Behaviour*, Penguin, 1972.
Bales, R. F., *Interaction Process Analysis: a method for the study of small groups*, Addison Wesley, Cambridge, Mass. 1950.
Bales, R. F., 'The Equilibrium Problem in Small Groups', in Parsons, T., Bales, R. F., and Shils, E. A., *Working Papers in the Theory of Action*, Free Press, Glencoe, IV. 1953.
Douglas, A., *Industrial Peacemaking*, Columbia University Press, 1962.
Dyar, D. A., 'Industrial Relations Training: Developing Short Courses in Negotiation.' *Industrial Training International*, vol. 8, no. 8, August 1973.
Hare, A. P., *Handbook of Small Group Research*, The Free Press, N.Y. 1962.
Klein, J., *Working with Groups*, Hutchinson University Library, London 1963.
Landsberger, H. A., 'Interaction Process Analysis of the Mediation of Management of Disputes.' *Journal of Abnormal and Social Psychology*, 1955.
NIIP, *Interviewing for Selection* (1972) and *The Seven Point Plan* (1970), National Institute of Industrial Psychology.
Rackham, N., *Development and Evaluation of Supervisory Training*, Research Report 71/1, Air Transport and Travel Industry Training Board, Staines, Middlesex 1971.
Rackham, N., 'Developing Negotiation Skills', *Industrial and Commercial Training*, vol. 4, no. 6, 1972.
Rackham, N., Honey, P., and Colbert, M., *Developing Interactive Skills*, Wellens, 1971.
Stephenson, G. M., 'Inter-group Relations and Negotiation Behaviour', in Warr, P. B. (ed.), *Psychology at Work*, Penguin, 1971.
Stephenson, G., and Morley, I., Proceedings of British Psychological Society, Social Psychology Section, Durham University, 1970.
Stewart, R., *Managers and their Jobs*, Macmillan, 1967.
Warr, P., Bird, M., and Rackham, N., *Evaluation of Management Training*, Gower Press, London 1970.

4 Assertiveness training

Sandra V. Langrish

The assertive person, as described by Alberti and Emmons in *Your Perfect Right* (1970), is '. . . open and flexible, genuinely concerned with the rights of others, yet at the same time able to establish very well his own rights'

A central belief of assertiveness training is that:

each person should be able to choose for himself how he will act in a given circumstance. If his 'polite restraint' response is too well developed he may be unable to make the choice to act as he would like to. If his aggressive response is overdeveloped, he may be unable to achieve his own goals without hurting others. (Alberti and Emmons, 1970)

In *Your Perfect Right* the authors identified three contrasting modes of behaviour. These are:

non-assertive behaviour – denying one's own rights
aggressive behaviour – denying the rights of others
assertive behaviour – acknowledging your own rights and those of others.

Examples of each mode will give a clearer picture of how they operate in life. Imagine, for example, you are working on a project. It is 4.30 pm and you have arranged to meet a friend at 5.00 so that you can go for a meal and a theatre visit together. Your boss rushes into your office waving a piece of paper. He has just received a telephone call about some aspect of the project which requires the preparation of an additional document '. . . right now!' You realise it will take you until at least 5.45 to do the work. What do you say?

Non-assertive response: 'That's OK. I'll drop what I'm doing and do it right now. Just leave it with me. I'll take care of it.'

Aggressive response: 'What do you take me for? Do you think I've got nothing better to do than jump when you whistle? Well, if you do, you've got a big shock coming! I'm going out with a friend, and I'm leaving at 5.00 on the dot. Just find someone else to run after you.'

Assertive response: 'I realise that it's important that this is done as soon as possible but I've made arrangements to meet a friend at 5.00, so I can't do it now. However, I'll do it first thing tomorrow.'

This fictional incident illustrates a number of aspects of assertiveness theory which are based upon the premise that every individual possesses certain basic human rights, and that the *goal* of assertiveness should be to stand up for one's basic human rights without violating the human rights of others. These rights include such fundamentals as:

the right to make mistakes
the right to set one's own priorities
the right to have one's own needs be as important as the needs of other people
the right to refuse requests without having to feel guilty or selfish
the right to express ourselves as long as we don't violate the rights of others
the right to judge our own behaviour, thoughts and emotions, and to take responsibility for the consequences.

In the incident described above the *non-assertive* person has permitted her own rights to be violated by failing to refuse an unreasonable request. The *aggressive* person has punished her boss by trying to make him feel guilty and responsible for trying to spoil her evening. The *assertive* person has acknowledged the other person's right to ask her to do extra work, but has stuck by the arrangements she has previously made, and has thereby refused to have her own rights violated. In addition, by offering to do the work first thing the following morning, she has suggested a reasonable compromise arrangement.

70

A further refinement has been made by Phelps and Austin (*The Assertive Woman*, 1975) of the three general classifications of behaviour suggested by Alberti and Emmons (1970). They have subdivided the aggressive mode into two parts: direct aggression and indirect aggression. As direct aggression is culturally disapproved for women, they frequently attempt to hide or mask their aggression by indirect aggression. This behaviour can apply equally to men, but is more frequently displayed by women, who learn to get what they want by indirect means and show aggression or hostility indirectly, as they are unable to confront others directly with their anger. They resort to sulking, silence, lack of eye contact and showing their resentment and hostility through facial expression and general demeanour.

An indirectly aggressive woman, when faced with an unreasonable request such as the one described earlier, would reply verbally in similar terms to the non-assertive person. However, she would also sulk, pout, slam drawers and generally indicate her displeasure indirectly, possibly culminating in slapping down the completed work on the manager's desk with a remark such as, 'Well, here it is. I missed a night out because of you – I hope you're happy'.

Indirect aggression leads to feelings of frustration and may turn ultimately into direct aggression. By resorting to indirect aggression first, the person increases his or her feelings of powerlessness.

Aggression, both direct and indirect, and non-assertiveness result in communication breakdowns between individuals. This reduces the effectiveness of work teams as honest communication becomes impossible, and this has serious effects upon individuals, work groups and organisations. As Hersey and Blanchard (1977) point out, 'Our greatest failure as human beings has been the inability to secure cooperation and understanding with others'. Assertive behaviour can give us the skills we need to overcome this failing.

Assertiveness training methods have largely been developed in the United States, but are equally applicable in this country. Training programmes have been used both in personal counselling and in helping individuals to be more effective in the workplace. It is increasingly seen as an effective method of training in interpersonal and inter-group skills because it concentrates upon changing behaviour. The theoretical framework described above is used as a basis for the teaching of specific skills which are practised in the relatively non-threatening environment of the training session and can then be transferred to the workplace.

71

An important issue which needs to be identified and confronted early in any training programme is the problem of distinguishing between *assertive* and *aggressive* behaviour. These two terms are frequently confused, and assertive behaviour may be thought to mean being aggressive, bossy and domineering. However, the Oxford English Dictionary defines 'assertive' as 'The action of stating positively, declaring or claiming'. Assertive behaviour is open, honest and non-manipulative, and involves the 'direct expression of one's feelings, preferences, needs or opinions in a manner that is neither threatening nor punishing towards the other person' (Galassi and Galassi, 1977).

In the workplace, both aggressive and non-assertive behaviour can be counter-productive, as they reduce the chance of effectively accomplishing work goals, and also have negative consequences for individuals. The *goal* of assertiveness training is thus not only to enable the individual to learn to interact more effectively with others and to feel okay about himself, but also to be a more effective member of the work team.

An assertiveness training programme concentrates upon developing a number of specific *skill* areas. These include:

the ability to cope with manipulation and criticism without responding with counter-criticism, counter-manipulation or withdrawing with hurt feelings, guilt or shame;
the ability to make requests and state points of view in a confident, straightforward manner without getting loud, annoyed or angry;
the ability to co-operate with others in solving problems in an adult way so that both parties share the thinking process and get most of what they want.

The *design* of an assertiveness training programme must be geared to the needs of the target population. For example, a staff development programme will differ from individual counselling in terms of methods, structure and areas of experience to be examined. Nevertheless, it is possible to suggest a structure and methods which could be adapted for use in a variety of environments. A programme must include:

the basic theory and philosophy of assertiveness training;
recognition of non-assertion, indirect aggression and assertion in oneself and others;
identification of personal assertiveness training needs;
rehearsal and role play of assertiveness skills in the areas of personal need;

practice of rehearsed behaviours in the 'back-home' environment; evaluation of behaviour in everyday interactions.

In Figure 4.1 it is possible to see the way in which the programme can

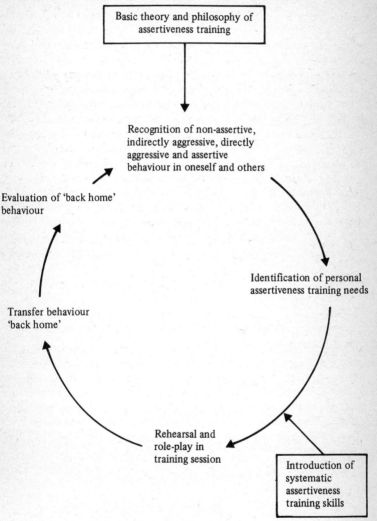

Fig. 4.1   Assertiveness training — components of programme

operate over time to meet successive areas of training need. The major instruments used in this programme are:

1 The assertion self-assessment table (Figure 4.2)
2 The assertive behaviour hierarchy (Figure 4.3)
3 The daily log of assertive behaviour (Figure 4.4).

Stage 1: Assertion self-assessment table

Along the left-hand side of the grid there are row headings which list a variety of *activities* that represent the major categories of assertiveness: expression of positive feelings, expression of self-affirmation and expression of negative feelings. The column headings list *people* to whom these activities may be addressed. The people represented are not inclusive of all people with whom one may interact, and a choice must be made of the individuals who are most relevant for oneself.

To assess the level of assertiveness in each activity ask yourself, 'To what extent do I feel comfortable carrying out this activity with this person?' For example, if you begin with the upper left-hand cell you would form the question, 'Do I feel comfortable giving compliments to friends of the same sex as myself?' If the answer is 'yes', enter a tick in the cell; if the answer is 'no', enter a cross. Continue in this manner for all the cells of the grid. Completion of the table permits the identification of those people and activities with which you have difficulty in behaving assertively.

Stage 2: Assertive behaviour hierarchy

From the information gained from Figure 4.2 it is possible to construct an assertive behaviour hierarchy (Figure 4.3). To construct the hierarchy, select as the first item a person or activity which you feel you could handle assertively with only minimal anxiety. Continue to order the items from least anxiety-provoking to most anxiety-provoking. The last item should be the people and activities which cause you the greatest anxiety and discomfort.

Once the hierarchy has been constructed, it permits the identification of both long term and short term personally assessed training goals which range from the easiest to the most difficult. It may be found that people fall into categories such as 'authority figures', and activities into similar groupings such as 'learning to say no' to unreasonable requests. In this case it will be found that during training,

PEOPLE

ACTIVITY	Friends of the same sex	Friends of the opposite sex	Intimate relations, e.g. spouse, boyfriend, girlfriend	Parents, in-laws, and other family members	Children	Authority figures, e.g. bosses, professors, doctors	Business contacts, e.g. sales-persons, waiters	Co-workers, colleagues, and subordinates
Expressing positive feelings								
Give compliments								
Receive compliments								
Express liking, love, and affection								
Make requests, e.g. ask for favours, help, etc.								
Touch affectionately								
Initiate and maintain conversations								
Self-affirmation								
Stand up for your legitimate rights								
Refuse requests								
Refuse invitations								
Express personal opinions, including disagreement								
Expressing negative feelings								
Express justified annoyance and displeasure								
Express justified anger								

Adapted from Galassi, M.D. and Galassi, J.P., *Assert Yourself*, Human Sciences Press, 1977.

Fig. 4.2   Assertion self-assessment table

1

2

3

4

5

6

7

8

9

10

Fig. 4.3   Your own assertive behaviour hierarchy

improving behaviour in one setting may have a spin-off with related behaviours and people.

Stage 3: Introduction of systematic assertiveness training skills

These skills are of two main kinds:

1 Verbal skills
2 Non-verbal skills.

The *verbal skills* have been outlined by Manuel J. Smith in *When I say no, I feel guilty* (1975), and include:

Broken record — a skill that by calm repetition — saying what you want over and over again — teaches persistence and permits you to ignore manipulative verbal side traps, argumentative baiting and irrelevant logic, whilst sticking to your desired point, and is particularly effective with persistent salesmen.

Fogging — a skill that teaches the acceptance of manipulative criticism by calmly acknowledging to your critic the probability that there may be some truth in what he/she says, yet allows you to remain your own judge of what you do. It allows you to receive criticism comfortably without becoming anxious or defensive.

Free information and self-disclosure — skills that teach the recognition of simple cues given by a social partner in everyday conversation to indicate what is interesting or important to that person, together with the initiation and maintenance of social interactions. This is most effective in promoting closer personal relationships.

Negative assertion — a skill that teaches acceptance of your errors and faults (without having to apologise) by strongly and sympathetically agreeing with hostile or constructive criticism of your negative qualities. It permits you to look more comfortably at negatives in your own behaviour without feeling defensive and anxious or resorting to denial of real errors.

Negative inquiry — a skill that teaches the active prompting of criticism in order to use the information (if helpful) or exhaust it (if manipulative), whilst prompting your critic to be more assertive, less dependent on manipulative ploys. It encourages the other person to express honest negative feelings and improves communication.

Workable compromise — whenever you feel your self-respect is not in question it is useful to offer a workable compromise to the other person. However, if the end goal involves a matter of your self-worth, there can be no compromise.

Recognition of the *non-verbal* content of assertive, non-assertive and aggressive behaviour is an important area of learning which facilitates behaviour change.

When being *assertive*, a person generally establishes good eye contact, stands or sits comfortably without fidgeting and talks in a strong, steady voice, neither shouting nor numbling. Assertive words include 'I' statements such as 'I think', 'I feel', 'I want', co-operative words such as 'let's, or 'we could', and empathetic statements of interest such as 'what do you think', 'how do you feel'.

A *non-assertive* response is self-effacing and may be accompanied by such mannerisms as the shifting of weight, downcast eyes, a slumped body posture or a hesitant, giggly or whining voice. Non-assertive words can include qualifiers such as 'maybe', 'I wonder if you could', 'only', 'just', 'would you mind very much', 'I can't', or fillers such as 'you know', 'well', 'uh', and negators: 'it's not really important', 'it's all right', 'don't bother'.

An *aggressive* response is typically expressed by inappropriate anger

77

or hostility which is loudly and explosively expressed. It is characterised by glaring eyes, leaning forward or pointing a finger, and an angry tone of voice. Aggressive words include threats such as 'you'd better' or 'if you don't watch out', put-downs such as 'come *on*', or 'you must be kidding', and evaluative comment such as 'should', 'I thought you'd know better'. *Indirectly aggressive* behaviour uses the language of the non-assertive response combined with the non-verbal behaviour of the aggressive mode, concentrating upon body posture and angry movements.

Stage 4: Rehearsal and role play

The essence of assertiveness training is its practical orientation which emphasises that 'head knowledge' is an essential starting point for behaviour change, but must be followed by personal involvement in rehearsing desired changes in behaviour.

Using the individually-constructed assertive behaviour hierarchy (Figure 4.3), a particular problem is selected from the top of the hierarchy. The trainer then role plays this with the trainee.

Typically, the initial performance is not assertive, and the trainer and other group members will give feed-back on verbal and non-verbal content of the trainee's assertiveness. From this the trainee can modify and change his behaviour until he feels that he is performing at a level of assertiveness which is comfortable for him.

In the early stages of a programme it may require more than one rehearsal and role-play session before a satisfactory level of assertiveness is attained for a particular problem.

Friends and relations may help with rehearsal and role-play sessions, provided, of course, that they don't feature prominently in the hierarchy as problems themselves.

The trainer's role is primarily that of facilitator and coach, encouraging the identification of realistic levels of performance and encouraging the recognition and rehearsal of assertive behaviour.

Stage 5: Transfer of behaviour 'back home'

When the performance is satisfactory, the behaviour is then transferred back into the workplace into daily interactions. During the training period a log of assertiveness behaviour (Figure 4.4) is kept. Effectiveness in interactions is measured by assessing the degree of eye contact, posture, appropriate facial expression and verbal performance.

Date	What I did	Person	Satisfactory aspects of performance	Aspects of performance that need improvement	Overall evaluation excellent/good/ fair/poor

Fig. 4.4   Daily log of assertive behaviour

The stages of the cycle are then repeated for the next item on the hierarchy. This programme enables assertiveness in a variety of interactions from the least threatening to the most threatening to be improved.

Assertiveness training is a technique which trainees can use to improve their social effectiveness in the workplace. It has a body of theory which must be inderstood initially by trainees, but as this is followed by an individually determined training programme it is an effective means of bringing about changes in behaviour. In addition, the self-monitoring of performance increases the individual's sense of autonomy and control over his own life which results in the reduction of feelings of powerlessness. Assertiveness training is an ideal tool for personal development and increasing effectiveness.

References

Alberti, R. E., and Emmons, M. L., *Your Perfect Right: a Guide to Assertive Behaviour*, Impact, 1970.

Galassi, M. D., and Galassi, J. P., *Assert Yourself! How to be Your Own Person*, Human Science Press, 1977.

Hersey, P., and Blanchard, K. H., *Management of Organisational Behaviour*, Prentice-Hall, 1977.

Phelps, S., and Austin, N., *The Assertive Woman,* Impact, 1975.

Smith, M. J., *When I Say No, I Feel Guilty*, Bantam Books, 1975.

5 The T-group approach

Peter B. Smith

Introduction

'T-group training' is a phrase used to describe a training method whose
purpose is to increase the trainee's skills in working with other people.
The method differs from other available methods in that trainees spend
a considerable proportion of their time talking about their relationships
with each other on the training course. The usefulness of the T-group
method needs to be assessed in relation to the other methods such as
discussion groups, syndicate groups and case study which have been
used for the same purpose. Experience with these methods indicates
three major areas in which there is scope for improvement:

1 Such training has often been based on prescriptions that a particular pattern of behaviour was the most effective in all circumstances. On the contrary, research has shown that the effectiveness
of, for example, a style of leadership, depends on the environment
within which it is performed.
2 Such training has often been abstract and diffuse, concerned
with generalisations about people in general and consequently
inapplicable to many of the individual trainees.
3 Such training has emphasised the benefits of participative

approaches to problem-solving and management, without acknowledging that in some circumstances these benefits are outweighed by other disadvantages.

T-group training attempts to overcome each of these difficulties. Groups of trainees are encouraged to talk specifically about one another's behaviour. In doing so they avoid the abstract. By discussing together the consequences of their having behaved in particular ways, they transform prescribed learning into something which each person learns from experience for himself. As we shall see, the method does not lay down that trainees should adopt more participative styles of management; it is equally likely that a trainee may learn from his group to be more aggressive rather than less so. Any changes would be the result of a complex inter-play between the trainee's own goals and the reactions he gets from the group when he behaves in different ways.

It is difficult for some people to visualise what a group of trainees could possibly find to talk about for long periods, with only their own relationships as agenda. The prospect sounds as though it would be either embarrassing, boring or alarming. Most trainees do experience each of these reactions at some time or other during training, but they tend to be outweighed by interest and involvement.

It may help to clarify the task of the T-group if we consider a simple model of the different types of behaviour found in a group. This is shown in Figure 5.1.

A good deal of behaviour in a group falls within the 'public' area, that is to say it is behaviour of which everyone is aware. This would include who is sitting where, who is speaking, what is being discussed and so forth. However, some behaviour is 'blind', in the sense that a person who is behaving in a particular way is unaware of the effect it is having. One may be unaware of gestures one is using or the overtones of what one is saying, which other group members nonetheless pick up. A task of the T-group is to help members to reduce their blind area. Other behaviour in the group is 'hidden', in the sense that a group member decides that he or she does not wish to communicate on particular issues to other group members, so that others remain unaware of them. This would include organisational secrets, personal fears and aspects of relationships outside the group. A second task of the group is for members to test out whether they hide too much or too little from others. If they conceal too much others will develop a misleading image of them, which they may not like. If they reveal what

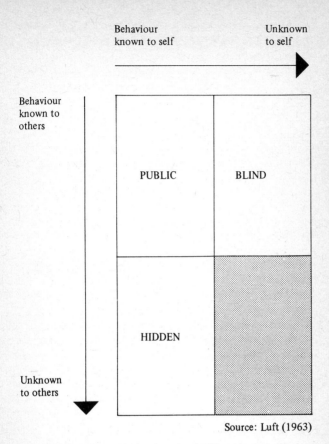

Fig. 5.1   Classification of behaviour in the T-group

others do not want to know, they may also find it more difficult to get on well with them. The shaded area at the bottom right of Figure 5.1 is both 'blind' and 'hidden' and is usually referred to as 'unconscious'. It is not part of the usual task of the T-group to explore it.

The usual effect of a T-group is to enlarge the public area, and somewhat to reduce the 'blind' and 'hidden' areas.

T-group methods differ quite markedly from other approaches to training. In this chapter we shall begin by looking at groups composed of trainees who are initially strangers to one another and are drawn from a range of different organisations. We shall then turn to modifications of the T-group for use within single organisations and workgroups. The goals of the stranger T-group and the organisational T-group are quite different. What links them together is the central theme of this chapter – a group of trainees discussing their own relationships.

The training method

The phrase 'T-group' stands only for 'training-group', so it is particularly uninformative. The method is also referred to as sensitivity training, laboratory training and group relations training. Where we are concerned with groups of strangers, this type of training has three goals:

1 Increases in sensitivity – the ability to perceive accurately how others are reacting to one's own behaviour.
2 Increases in diagnostic ability – the ability to perceive accurately the state of relationships between others.
3 Increases in action skill – the ability to carry out skilfully the behaviour required by the situation. Action skill implies the ability to carry out a range of different behaviours and thus requires flexibility in choosing the right behaviour from a range of possible behaviours.

In order to understand how participation in a T-group might facilitate progress towards these goals, we shall consider the development of a typical T-group from the viewpoint of the trainer and examine the ways in which he or she attempts to encourage the favoured outcomes. In later sections the emphasis will be on testing the effectiveness of these attempts against independent research evidence.

The development of the T-group

A T-group usually contains between seven and a dozen trainees with one or two staff trainers. They meet for periods of three to five days, although some groups last up to ten days. During this time the principal activity, though by no means the only one, is meetings of the T-group. The group meets in a residential centre, away from everyday distractions. The first day or two in the life of the group is crucial to the success of the training, since during this time the group has to 'learn how to learn' in a novel way. Let us follow their attempts.

The first T-group session is started by the staff trainer who explains the goals and meeting times of the group. He most likely indicates his willingness to help the group learn from examination of their own behaviour, but he does not specify precisely how this might be achieved. His contributions to the session thereafter tend to be infrequent. Group members attempt to get discussion going on a variety of topics but find this difficult to sustain. By the end of the session it is likely that some members of the group will have attempted to discuss or comment on the behaviour of others in the group or the group as a whole. The trainer may encourage such discussion and contribute his own reactions, but in any event the discussion is short-lived. The position in the group at this time can be visualised as in Figure 5.2.

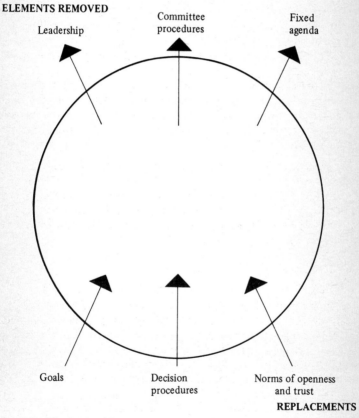

ELEMENTS REMOVED

Leadership

Committee procedures

Fixed agenda

Goals

Decision procedures

Norms of openness and trust

REPLACEMENTS

Fig. 5.2 The leadership vacuum

The trainer has declined to provide the strong lead that might be expected of the leader. There are no agreed procedures for replacing the leader nor is there an agenda of topics to discuss. Until the group can invent acceptable replacements to fill the vacuum, it is a tense and uncomfortable place to be. The newly emergent structure will be one that takes account of the goals of both group members and trainer; it will provide a climate where the group are sufficiently trusting of one another to be able to discuss their behaviour.

The process whereby the climate of a T-group develops is only partially understood. Many people describe the T-group as 'unstructured' but this is certainly inaccurate; there is considerable consistency between the climate that develops in different groups. This consistency is not coincidence, but is the outcome of some of the inherent factors in the situation, such as the trainer's goals and behaviour, the duration of the course and the common needs of many trainees. The group then is structured, but it is structured in an unusual way.

As meetings of the T-group proceed, the point is quickly reached where group members address themselves to one another by giving 'feedback' or expressing their reactions to one another. It soon emerges that to give feedback to someone is not to guarantee that they will find it acceptable. The are equally likely to explain with some exasperation how they are not at all like how other people say they are. Our experiences have left most of us with some certainty as to what sort of people we are, and we are unlikely to abandon such a self-concept because somebody in a T-group sees us in another light. The T-group member needs to learn that while the self-concept no doubt accurately describes some aspects of oneself, it leaves out of account other aspects of which one is unaware.

In the course of their development most T-groups incorporate more of the 'hidden' and 'blind' areas (see Figure 5.1) into the area of 'public knowledge' within the group. If group members can understand how certain aspects of their behaviour are blind to them, they are well on the way to achieving the goals listed earlier (i.e. increases in sensitivity, diagnostic ability and action skill). The acceptance or rejection of feedback in the T-group depends largely on the level of trust there is in the group. This leads to some crucial questions as to how the T-group achieves what it does, which we shall explore presently. For the moment, it shall suffice to say that group members trust one another where they know they are in a position to hurt or exploit one another and yet they do not do so. This situation is likely to arise for example

86

where someone reveals something from his or her hidden area.

The time of the T-group is thus given over to the expression and receipt of feedback between group members. It is easy to see how quick and accurate feedback about events in the group can lead to increases in sensitivity and in diagnostic ability of the trainee. The action skill component is concerned with the expression of verbal statements at appropriate times. The working lives of most managers contain a heavy component of talking to others, whether to seek information, persuade, command, enlist their support or give information. So it is in the T-group. Each member has opportunities to test out and develop personal behavioural skills, where situations arise in the group requiring such skills.

Training design

The T-group provides the major component of any T-group course, or laboratory as it is often called. One of the skills required of T-group trainers is that of planning and conducting a variety of supporting activities whose purpose is to enhance the effectiveness of the T-group as a learning situation. These supporting activities vary considerably both with the training needs of a particular population and with the skills and predilections of the trainer. Some of the more widely used elements of design are listed in Figure 5.3, along with the purposes for which they are included.

This variability of design poses problems when one begins assessing the effectiveness of T-group training, since it becomes less easy to specify the precise cause of any effects of training which are detected. These problems are not acute, however, since the majority of the design elements in Figure 5.3 incorporate the basic method of the T-group, namely examination of actual behaviour as it happens. The exceptions to this — lectures and application groups — tend not to be highly valued by participants, although there may be cogent reasons for retaining them.

Intergroup exercises are one of the elements of laboratory design which often receives a relatively heavy time allocation. In an intergroup exercise the members of each T-group will be asked, for example, to prepare a plan of how to use a subsequent part of the laboratory or to prepare a presentation of their own group's history or culture. Subsequent interaction with the other groups highlights the dynamics of intergroup relationships. The effect of intergroup exercises on each T-

ELEMENT	PURPOSE
Lectures	Intellectual clarification of problems in group and organisational behaviour.
Intergroup observation	To see similarities and differences in the way different groups face up to common issues.
Paired discussion	Practice: (1) in helping someone else to obtain benefit from their T-group; (2) in receiving such help.
Non-verbal exercises	Extension of T-group to examine interpersonal communication other than by word of mouth.
Intergroup exercises	Extension of T-group learning to problems of representation, negotiation and conflict management.
Application groups	To facilitate the transfer of what has been learned to the trainee's actual job behaviour.
Group recomposition	To bring together trainees who may be particularly able to learn from one another.
Research data collection	Monitoring the success of the laboratory, plus making a contribution to long-term development of the method.

Fig. 5.3   Laboratory design elements

group is considerable so that some care is necessary in scheduling such an exercise at a time when the T-groups are not preoccupied with relationships among themselves.

Application groups are often composed of trainees whose job background is as similar as possible, in contrast to the T-groups where the training staff attempt to make the groups relatively heterogeneous. The task of the application group is to explore the ways in which members plan to apply what they have learned to their job performance. This may involve them in detailed discussion and diagnosis of their specific job situations as well as a more detached analysis of what it is that they have learned during the laboratory. Application groups are more effective when they have four to six members rather than more. Naturally, their meetings are scheduled more toward the end of the laboratory. It is not surprising that many trainees find it difficult to see benefit in their application groups. The T-group provides the central focus of the laboratory, and yet the application group asks the participant to step back from what may be an intense involvement in his T-group and contemplate, in a detached way, possible responses to his behaving in a changed way when he returns to his job. Such a transfer must in the end happen and if application groups help trainees to anticipate it, they will be of value.

Varieties of training design

The various elements of training design described in the preceding paragraphs all assume that the central element in the design is a series of T-group meetings. In practice further design options are open to the trainer in which the central element has a somewhat different character. Three such options are provided by the encounter group, the Tavistock study group and programmes of structured exercises. Since each of these overlap to some extent with T-groups, and are sometimes confused with them, they will be briefly described.

Encounter groups arose in the 1960s through the feeling of some T-group leaders that the development of T-groups was more aimless and slow-moving than it need be (Schutz, 1973). They therefore devised a style of group leadership which was more directive and controlling, and which provided group members with firm guidance towards the exploration of their most basic emotional orientations towards others. This approach led to the development of hundreds of different 'non-verbal activities' through which group members express their feelings about themselves, and others, not verbally but through some form of physical activity. Examples of those frequently employed are where a member seeks to push him or herself into a group from which they feel excluded, and where one person guides another on a 'blind' walk. The first of these is intended to facilitate exploration of feelings of exclusion and how one copes with them. The second opens up one's feelings about giving and receiving help. Encounter groups have acquired for themselves a somewhat gaudy image, reflecting the undoubted excesses of some practitioners. The difficulty is that the term is currently used by some group leaders (e.g. Rogers, 1971) whose approach is close to that of many T-group leaders and by others whose style is a great deal more directive. Non-verbal activities have been utilised by many T-group leaders in recent years, but they tend to be employed sparingly and in the context of an ongoing T-group rather than as a way of making things happen. The more directive forms of encounter derive from Perls' gestalt therapy (Fagan and Shepherd, 1972) and psychodrama (Blatner, 1973).

In each of these approaches the leader actively structures the group experience. In gestalt therapy the work of the group is most usually conducted between the leader and just one of the group members at any one time. While the remaining group members observe, the member in the 'hot seat' carries through activities such as the role playing of different facets of a dream or of different parts of himself. The gestalt therapist structures the framework of the interchange, but not of course the actual feelings expressed by the member. Psychodrama, which was devised more than fifty years ago by Moreno, is in some ways similar, but utilises role-plays which involve several members concurrently. Psychodrama focuses more frequently on portraying family group dynamics, past or present, but the technique may be adapted to the portrayal of any situation. Still other techniques employed by some encounter leaders such as bioenergetics and massage are more relevant to one's awareness of one's body and therefore contrast with the interpersonal emphasis of most designs.

The Tavistock study group (e.g. Rice, 1965) is often seen as the characteristically English form of group work. Tavistock study groups differ from T-groups in that Tavistock leaders see their role as interpretive. Tavistock leaders remain apart from the group, defining their role as the interpretation of whatever occurs. By contrast T-group leaders are much more likely to be willing to join in with the group on an equal basis. The predictable effect of this is that Tavistock groups tend to be much more focused on issues of relationship to authority, whereas T-groups tend to be focused more often on relationships between equals.

Programmes of structured exercises also seek to provide the learning derivable from T-groups in a more directive manner. These differ from the more structured forms of encounter in that they specify not only the framework of learning but also what is to be learned. Some programmes seek to teach new ways of diagnosing behaviour in groups, such as, for instance, the managerial grid (Blake and Mouton, 1978), interaction analysis (Dyar and Giles, in Chapter 3 of this book), and transactional analysis (Berne, 1963). Details of many others are available in the annual series edited by Pfeiffer and Jones. Structured exercises are quite frequently employed by T-group leaders where the goals of a particular programme are focused with sufficient precision that they may be employed.

Using groups within the organisation

It was long thought that one of the prerequisites for the success of the T-group was separation from the different levels of authority existing within an organisation. It was argued that within the organisation it was inconceivable that people should feel free to speak openly and to develop the characteristic climate of the T-group.

While there is some force in this point of view, it remains true that fruitful methods have been developed of introducing modifications of T-group method within organisations. It is not so much a question of transplanting an innovation into the organisation, more a question of tailoring the training method to suit the particular circumstance of an organisation. In a 'stranger' T-group, members of the group develop a climate of trust in one another in order to increase certain skills. In an 'in-organisation' T-group a certain climate of relationships is already likely to exist and discussion of that climate is used either to modify it or to enable particular organisational goals to be clarified or achieved. The methods of in-organisation training remain relatively constant while the goals must vary with the circumstance.

We shall illustrate this variety by quoting a range of examples, including whatever research findings are available in specific instances.

Tailor-made programmes

Since many programmes of organisation development do not yield quantitative research data I shall first briefly summarise some British examples and then turn to more fully-researched instances. Figure 5.4 shows a representative sample. Since different programmes have different goals, there can be no question of an overall assessment of the use of groups within organisations. It may very well be that some usages are effective while others are ill-conceived or poorly executed. One can only hope to show that T-groups can be usefully employed within the organisation, not that they are always useful. A further point to bear in mind is that as one makes ever greater modifications in the nature of the T-group it becomes more difficult to distinguish it from other forms of intervention.

Almost all of the published research studies which exist concerning the use of T-groups within organisations detected changes greater than those obtained among controls not participating in the groups. Some of these changes were a good deal less radical, however, than had been hoped for.

91

TRAINING GOAL	PUBLISHED REFERENCE	BRIEF SUMMARY OF TRAINING DESIGN
Reduction of stereotypes between different functions (production, sales marketing)	Beckhard (1969)	1 Senior men participate in stranger groups and then agree to: 2 'Diagonal slice' groups (i.e. slice across the organisation chart, so that immediate superiors and subordinates are separated) examine the basis of their images of different functions
Development of teamwork in hotels	Beckhard (1966)	Periodic meetings with team
Facilitation of change in large industrial plant	Harrison (1972)	Three-phase training programme
Reallocation of roles in automated tankers	Hjelholt: reported in Clark (1972)	Appointed officers and crew meet with trainer shortly before tankers are launched Follow-up meetings
Team development in a management group	Mangham (1972)	In-company team T-group
Facilitating a merger	Mangham (1973)	Groups share images of one another
Contribution to course-work of management students	Reynolds (1976)	Experiential study of course as an organisation

Fig. 5.4   Instances of in-organisation group training

Perhaps the most spectacular study is that by Marrow et al. (1967) which details the takeover of a pyjama manufacturing company in the United States and its transformation over several years from an autocratic organisation incurring heavy losses to a highly participative organisation making substantial profits. This was achieved through a whole range of interventions, but it was concluded that the use of T-groups was a central element in this success story. This case study is instructive in a number of ways. It illustrates the manner in which the newly developing technology of organisational development need not, indeed must not, rest solely on the use of T-groups. Within the organisation the use of T-groups is simply one option appropriate to certain goals and not to others. In learning more about the range of goals to which T-groups may contribute, the failures may be as interesting as the successes. A second point which the Marrow study illustrates is the length of time required for the creation of a major organisational change. Shorter term interventions may be appropriate in approaching more modest goals, but some of the reported failures of organisational development may derive from the fact that insufficient time and resources were put into a project.

Cooper and Oddie (1972) made a comparative study of the effects of social skill training and T-group training on cafeteria staff on the M1. Both training programmes achieved some effects, notably decreased labour turnover. The effects of the T-group programme were still detectable twelve months after training from ratings by customers of the service they had received, whereas the effects of social skill training were no longer apparent.

A further problem in detecting change is that training may lead to changes in how trainees conceptualise their current situation. For instance Zand et al. (1969) found that, after in-company T-groups, managers in an engineering company perceived less trust in their work groups. On the basis of responses to other parts of the questionnaire the researchers concluded that this meant not that there was in fact less trust in the work-groups but that the managers were now setting themselves more demanding standards as to what was an adequate level of trust.

The number of studies now available of group training within organisations makes it possible to attempt some analysis of the causes of success and failure. Friedlander (1967) suggested that trust may prove to be a key variable. He showed that, in his sample of groups within a research and development station of the US Army, trust did not increase but those T-groups which were already high on trust showed improved effectiveness on other criteria. Franklin (1976) surveyed a wide range of organisational development interventions including some based on T-groups. Success was found to be related to numerous factors including the level of support from top management, the diagnostic skills of the change agent, the specificity of the probem definition, the firm's economic position and so forth. An earlier study of the same data by Bowers (1973) suggested that T-groups had been less effective than some of the other interventions, but no data are given as to whether the T-group interventions were made under favourable or unfavourable circumstances, nor how long they lasted.

The managerial grid

While some organisational development consultants have found it appropriate to vary their interventions according to organisation climate, others have adopted a more normative view of organisational change. The best known of these approaches is Blake and Mouton's (1978) managerial grid. The managerial grid consists of a simple diagnostic framework provided to members of a group to aid them in describing one another's behaviour. The diagnoses are based on how much emphasis a manager gives to 'people' on the one hand and to 'production' on the other. Managerial grid training comprises a sequence of activities designed to utilise the impact of the T-group, as modified in the service of change within whole organisations. Smith and Honour (1969) made a study of the first phase of such a training programme, within a division of a British manufacturing company.

In phase one of grid training, heterogeneous groups are composed of trainees from within the company. The goal is to increase open discussion of each other's behaviour so as to create readiness for the second phase in which work teams meet as groups. Forty-nine trainees were compared with 51 untrained controls from another plant, matched for age and seniority. Questionnaires were completed before and four months after training. The trainees were also interviewed at various intervals after the training. Slightly over half the trainees reported improvement in various aspects of their relationship to their subordinates, whereas the subordinates who we might expect to be more objective, saw the changes in about a third of the instances. Changes were particularly noted in group meetings and committees within the company. The untrained managers showed much lower change rates. Overall the study confirmed that the predicted changes did occur, but only among a minority of those trained.

Conclusions

T-group methods are those in which a group of people discuss their own relationships with one another. The goals of the method are to achieve increases in the trainees' sensitivity, diagnostic ability, and action skill. Where such training is conducted with a group who are initially strangers to one another there is good evidence that it has a durable effect on many of those trained. The effect of training is enhanced where the group climate permits the 'internalisation' of learning. Factors favouring the development of internalisation during training are the genuineness or authenticity of the trainer, the appropriateness of the trainer's interventions to the T-group's culture, the design of the programme, discussion of the problems of transferring what is learned back to one's job, the composition of the group and probably the conditions on which the trainee enters training.

Where T-groups are used within a single organisation, their use is intended to achieve a variety of goals. No overall assessment of their effectiveness is possible, but for such training to be beneficial some level of trust must already exist in the groups before training. Grid training has also been shown to have some effect in this area.

References

Beckhard, R., 'An organisation improvement program in a decentralised organisation', *Journal of Applied Behavioural Science*, 1966, 2, pp. 3-26.

Beckhard, R., *Organisation development: strategies and models.* Addison-Wesley, Reading, Mass. 1969.

Berne, E., *The structure and dynamics of organisations and groups*, Lippincott, New York 1963.

Blake, R. R., and Mouton, J. S., *The new managerial grid*, Gulf Publishing Co., Houston 1978.

Blatner, H.A., *Acting In: practical applications of psychodramatic methods*, Springer, New York 1973.

Bowers, D. G., 'OD techniques and their results in 23 organisations', *Journal of Applied Behavioral Science*, 1973, 9, pp. 21-43.

Clark, P.A., *Action research and organisational change*, Harper Row, London 1972.

Cooper, C. L., and Oddie, H., 'An evaluation of two approaches to social skill training in the catering industry', Hotel and Catering Industry Training Board, London 1972.

Fagan, J., and Shepherd, I.L. (eds), *Gestalt Therapy Now*, Penguin, Harmondsworth 1972.

Franklin, J. L., 'Characteristics of successful and unsuccessful organisation development', *Journal of Applied Behavioral Science*, 1976, 12, pp. 471-92.

Friedlander, F., 'The impact of organisational training laboratories on the effectiveness and interaction of ongoing work groups', *Personal Psychology*, 1967, 20, pp. 289-307.

Harrison, K., 'Group training within an organisational development project in an industrial company' in C. L. Cooper (ed.) *Group training for individual and organisational change*, Karger, Basle 1972.

Luft, J., *Group Processes*, Palo Alto, California: National Press, 1963.

Mangham, I.L., 'Building an effective work team' in M. L. Berger and P. J. Berger (eds), *Group Training Techniques,* Gower Press, Epping 1972.

Mangham, I.L., 'Facilitating intraorganisational dialogue in a merger situation', *Interpersonal Development*, 1973, 4, pp. 133-47.

Marrow, A.J., Bowers, D.G., and Seashore, S.E., *Management by participation*, Harper Row, New York 1967.

Rice, A. K., *Learning for Leadership*, Tavistock, London 1965.

Rogers, C., *Encounter groups*, Penguin, Harmondsworth 1971.

Schutz, W.C., *Joy: expanding human awareness*, Penguin, Harmondsworth 1973.

Smith, P. B., and Honour, T. F., 'The impact of phase I managerial grid training', *Journal of Management Studies*, 1969, 6, pp. 318-30.

Zand, D.E., Steele, F. and Zalkind, S.S., 'The impact of an organisational development program on perceptions of interpersonal, group and organisation functioning', *Journal of Applied Behavioral Science*, 1969, 5, pp. 393-410.

6 A comparative evaluation

Cary L. Cooper

Managers are dealing increasingly with more and more complex 'people problems' in the course of their work (Cooper, 1979), which has led to an enormous growth in executive training and development in the human relations or social skills. Tens of thousands of managers each year are sent or volunteer for some form of experiential small group training programme, such as the T-group method. After over two decades of this type of executive training, concerned people are beginning to ask: 'what are the adverse and growthful effects of this training on the quality of executive life'; 'are managers showing improvements at work and home as a result of this substantial training initiative; and in particular 'what are the psychological *costs* of this training on the individual, his work colleagues, his family and the organisation'? Since experiential small group training has become one of the most important tools in attempting to improve the quality of work relationships of managers in organisations (in the West), it was felt that we should explore in depth a study carried out by the author, for the Training Services Division, into the positive and adverse effects of social skill training based on experiential small group methods, variations of which were discussed at the end of the last chapter.

97

Introduction

Small group experiential training has come to be seen as a significant method of management training and development, particularly over the last decade. One of the major reasons for this is the increased demand that managers be more flexible in their approach to manager-worker relationships. This arises from an increasing shift towards more participative management and government pressure for greater worker participation in decision making. As we move in the direction of being more work-group oriented, and away from the narrow objective of developing the individual manager in isolation, the problems associated with interpersonal relations and group dynamics must inevitably grow and become magnified.

The small group training approach offers one obvious method for the improvement of relationships in an organisation. It allows not only for the simulation of organisational situations and the examination of the task and process aspects of such simulations, but also a chance for people to drop their organisational 'roles', become more aware of their needs, and give others honest feedback: actions which might not be sanctioned in the formal organisational atmosphere.

As such, the group can be used to cross barriers in a particularly powerful way, especially in the area of feedback. This also means, though, that the power of the group may work to the detriment, as well as the benefit, of participants. A participant could be 'attacked' with severe feedback in a group situation, which would never have surfaced in the organisational situation. Given a particularly vulnerable person, this may be a damaging experience. The individual may receive negative feedback which entirely alters his self-view, maintained by his position in the organisational hierarchy.

The small group, therefore, offers itself as a powerful and useful method of inducing change in people, of increasing self-awareness through feedback and observation of oneself in different situations. By its very nature, one can postulate that it may be harmful to certain people under certain conditions, and the notion has increasingly been put forward that such group experiences can be psychologically dangerous.

Until recently, the backing for this negative viewpoint has been of an anecdotal nature, based on limited or circumscribed experiences. In the late 1960s the major questions concerning group training remained unanswered. There was no empirical evidence as to whether small, experiential training programmes (including the more extreme T-groups and encounter groups) were psychologically disturbing, and if they were, to what extent. Similarly, no data were available as to whether certain types of participants were more vulnerable in the group situation, and whether personality characteristics of trainers or specific group events were consistently related to stress. Since 1970 articles have begun to appear which employ a more controlled empirical approach to the subject. Their findings over the last six years have been quite divergent, and have divided into those studies which found significant negative effects and those which have found little evidence for such outcomes. Casualty rates have been reported of below 1 per cent and up to 16 per cent. There has been a great deal of evaluation research carried out assessing positive outcomes for managers, but very little on their negative consequences. Most of the studies which have been done have been those where the group participants were students.

Evaluating the effects of experiential management training

Against this background the Training Services Division funded a research programme by the author to study the psychological effects of small group training for managers. A number of small group training programmes were selected as the basis for research. These represented a number of the major approaches, from unstructured through to structured programmes. These were organised by five management consultancy organisations or other insititutions very well known for their work in experiential small group training in the United Kingdom. All the individual programmes of these five training organisations and institutions over an eighteen-month period were evaluated. The twelve programmes studied were organised on approximately a one-week residential basis, and had a number of important characteristics in common:

First, they were designed so that learning took place primarily in small groups, allowing a high level of participation, involvement and free communication.
Second, they were all to some extent or another 'process' as distinct from 'content' oriented. That is, the primary stress was on the feeling level of communications, rather than solely on the information or conceptual level.
Third, they were all oriented towards improving the human relations or social skills of managers as distinct from their task or technical skills.

99

All programmes, in one form or another, were attempting to provide the manager with a better understanding of the dynamics of social interaction, communications between people, social sensitivity, etc. The means they used to achieve some of these objectives were, however, very different, notably on some of the following dimensions: degree of structure of the experience, directiveness of trainer, balance of 'content' and 'process', level of interpersonal intimacy, degree of participant choice of learning tools, person versus group-centred orientations, etc. Some of the programmes were known to have a high degree of structure through pre-planned, time-linked exercises, while others were known to be relatively unstructured with a high degree of participative learning in the T-group style. Indeed, the programmes were selected because they represented a good cross-section of the small group training experiences for managers in the UK on these very dimensions. The subjects of the study were 227 male participants and 32 trainers in 12 management development training programmes using small group methods. The participants were middle to senior level managers from a variety of industrial organisations.

This chapter will summarise the research results of this particular study, because it represents one of the first attempts to assess both the positive and negative effects of one of the most influential tools of management development on the quality of executive life.

There were two basic questions we were attempting to answer in this research: 'To what extent does experiential small group training for managers produce negative and positive effects?' and 'What are the antecedent learning conditions that lead to these outcomes?'

We were particularly interested in the potentially damaging effects of these group experiences since (1) they are used quite extensively in industry (and their use is growing); (2) there has been a great deal of evaluation research (Bunker, 1965; Moscow, 1971) carried out to assess their positive outcomes for managers, but very little on their negative consequences; and finally (3) there has been a growing concern (Mann, 1970; Crawshaw, 1969) that these experiences produce an unacceptably high level of casualties by 'disrupting ongoing personality functions', 'encouraging inappropriate levels of intimacy which may destroy rewarding psychological relationships with other people' (particularly family, friends, and work colleagues) – thereby, impairing the quality of executive life.

In addition to evaluating the effectiveness, or lack thereof, of experiential small group training, we were concerned to try and identify

100

those process or learning dynamics that might contribute to potential damage or growth, in an effort to aid the training adviser in the use, design and execution of such training in the future. A third question we were also interested in answering, therefore, was 'what are the implications of this research for the conduct and implementation of small group training programmes for managers based on experiential learning techniques?'

Measures used in the research

In evaluating both the positive and negative effects of group training, we collected data about each participant from a variety of different sources: the trainee himself, other trainees, the trainer, family/friends, and work colleagues (boss, subordinates, and peers). Five central criteria of psychological disturbance or growth were used in the study to assess the effects of small group training: participant personality change (on the 16PF Inventory); self and other trainees' nominations of who were 'hurt' and 'helped' by the training, which Lieberman, Yalom and Miles (1973) found to be the best predictor of disturbance as judged by clinicians; trainer nomination of 'hurt' and 'helped', family and friends report on the participants' personal relationships and behaviour at six weeks and seven months after training; and work colleagues report on the impact of the training on work performance and work relationships at six weeks and seven months after training. [1] After considering the outcome effects of small group training programmes in terms of psychological damage or growth, we also focused on the learning conditions which may be contributing to the reported positive or negative change. Information was collected on five main antecedent learning conditions which could contribute to damage or growth: participant personality predispositions (as measured by the 16PF); trainer style as measured by participants' perception of trainer behaviour during the training; characteristics of type of group training programmes (e.g. level of intimacy, confrontation, degree of structure, etc.), as judged by independent observers; trainer personality (as measured by the 16PF); and participants' conditions of participation or reasons for attending the training (e.g. forced to attend, advised, self-selected, etc.).

The data collected were analysed on an overall basis (measure-by measure), on a group-by-group basis and on an individual basis (trying to identify individuals who had gained or suffered as a result of their group experience).

For purposes of allocating individual trainees into 'hurt' (at risk) and 'helped' (improved) categories, all participant scores were examined on all the criterion variables and if a participant showed significant or approaching significant change on three or more criteria in the same direction (positive or negative), he was considered either 'hurt' (at risk) or 'helped' as appropriate. In addition, the three criteria on which he changed had to be drawn from at least two different sources (e.g. family/friends' reports and 16PF change or work colleagues' report and peer nominations, etc.). Although this method of identification of individual cases of 'hurt' and 'helped' participants was arbitrary, it:

(a) provided us with corroborative criteria support, i.e. from two or more sources;
(b) allowed us to identify particular programmes which may be damaging or beneficial; and
(c) permitted us to highlight the processes or dynamics of these programmes once identified.

Adverse effects

In our study we found, in examining each trainee individually from all experiential small group training programmes investigated, that roughly 5 per cent or twelve participants could be identified as having a potentially negative experience (based on several independent criteria measures) or at the very most 10 per cent when based on only one criterion (a significantly negative report by a family member or friend or work colleague) on a short term basis (up to six weeks after training).

In addition, 11 per cent of the trainees were nominated by at least two of their fellow trainees at the end of the training as having been 'hurt' by the experience, while 19 per cent were placed in this category by at least one trainer. A follow-up examination of participants after seven months revealed that only four or 1.76 per cent (only one from the original twelve) could be clearly identified as sustaining negative effects (based on more than one criterion measure) or seven (3 per cent) if we include participants with only one negative evaluation by a family member, or friend or work colleague. Of participants identified as potentially 'at risk' six weeks after training, 91 per cent showed negative personality changes, 58 per cent were seen by family and friends as adversely affected, while only 8 per cent were reported by work colleagues as less effective at work.

The bulk of the negative reports from family and friends were not on 'relationship' scales (e.g. 'coping less well with personal and family relationships') but on scales related to the effect of the training on the 'person' of the trainee (e.g. he was 'emotionally affected'). That is, the individual trainee was seen as having had an impactful training experience but not necessarily one that was disruptive to significant 'relationships' at work or in the home. In addition, although nearly 33 per cent of participants were named by themselves or other trainees at least once as being 'hurt' by the experience, 67 per cent of these were also named at least twice as being 'helped'. It was also interesting to note, in this context, that of the original twelve participants designated as potentially 'hurt' by the experience at six weeks, seven of these showed marked significant improvement at seven months as judged by family, friends and *particularly* work colleagues.

It might be argued, therefore, that in the short term some kind of emotional reaction may be, *for a small number of participants*, a necessary precondition to long term change.

Comparison with previous studies

Having briefly explored the results on the possible extent of adverse effects of experiential groups it might be worthwhile putting these results into the context of previous work. There are only two studies which have found high casualty rates among participants in experiential groups. Gottschalk and Pattison (1969) reported that in a sample of three groups of 31 participants, there were eleven 'obviously acute pathological emotional reactions' (six of these occurred in a single group). The symptoms they noted among the eleven casualties were psychotic reactions (two), acute anxiety and temporary departure from group (two), isolation and withdrawal reactions (four), depressive reactions (two), and sadistic-exhibitionist behaviour (one). The authors acknowledge that their groups may have been atypical and, in addition, that the effects may have been only transient since they were reporting on behaviour 'during' training.

Although their figure of 30 per cent adverse effects is very high, there are several aspects of this research we should take into account. First, the assessment of trainees was carried out on the completion of the training, so we don't know what the long term effect was, particularly in the participants' family and work environments. Second, the

103

judgements of pathological emotional reactions were made by the authors themselves, who were psychiatric clinicians, and there may be a tendency for psychiatrists to attribute greater clinical significance to training behaviour than is warranted. And, finally, behaviour such as 'isolation and withdrawal reactions' in a group context could have a quite different significance from that in a two-person psychotherapeutic interview (a situation these clinicians are more used to) (Smith, 1975).

The second study which found a relatively high proportion of casualties is the most widely publicised one by Lieberman, Yalom and Miles (1973), in which they claim 'no less than 9 per cent of participants in the 18 groups studied became casualties'. Immediately after the group experiences they reported something like 8 per cent casualties and 8 per cent negative changers (defined as such if they showed negative changes on three or more psychometric and ratings criteria), a total of 16 per cent. Six months after training they found a 10 per cent negative changers rate, for a total of 18 per cent.

There are several reasons why we should be cautious of these results as well. First, the random assignment of students to groups may have increased the risk of psychological disturbance. Second, the decision to categorise the 'suspect' students into 'casualties' was based on sub-jective criteria, that is, self-report by the students and the authors' judgements of 'psychological decompensation' and not on measurable observed behaviour. No evidence is given to validate the authors' judge-ments, as in the Gottschalk and Pattison study. Third, it is arguable that informing experiential group participants about the possibilities of 'con-siderable emotional upsets' before the start of the experience minimises the psychological risks to participants. It may, in fact, have the reverse effect of creating an expectation of intensive psychotherapy, which may not have been established without this intervention. Fourth, they had data which indicated that 23 per cent of their control group were negative changers immediately after training and 15 per cent six months later. This is as high, if not higher, than the experiential groups. Although we have to be cautious when drawing conclusions from this study, as we must from any large scale study in this field, it still provides evidence of casualties as a result of experiential training.

Our investigation found a much lower rate of adverse effects than the above two studies, from roughly 5 per cent just after training to less than 2 per cent seven months later. In addition, the majority of partici-pants showing negative effects up to six weeks after training were seen to change significantly in a positive direction seven months later.

104

Our results are more in line with those of other studies which show smaller casualty rates. Ross, Kligfeld and Whitman (1971), for example, carried out a survey in the city of Cincinnati, Ohio, a community with extensive experiential group activity. They sent questionnaires to 162 psychiatrists asking them to report any cases in which a patient's 'psychotic reactions or personality disorganisations, whether transient or long-lasting, seemed to be consequent to participation in non-structured groups (e.g. T-groups, etc.) in the preceding five years.' Of the 91 per cent of the psychiatrists who responded only 19 separate patients were reported as becoming psychotic or acutely disorganised after group training. The authors were given figures for numbers of persons participating in such groups over the preceding five years, which totalled 2,900. Thus, the 19 represented 0.66 per cent of the population thought to be 'at risk'. Of the participants thought to have been through T-groups (1,150 in all), 14 were identified as casualties, an adverse effect rate of 1.2 per cent. This is very close to the follow-up rate in our study.

In another study, Batchelder and Hardy (1968) carried out an evaluation of group training among 1,200 YMCA participants. Interviews with known critics of experiential small group training in the YMCA turned up four cases of allegedly severe adverse effect. After further in-depth work with these participants, trainers, work colleagues, etc., the authors came to the conclusion that in at least three cases the ultimate, long term outcome was beneficial rather than harmful. This is consistent with our follow-up data on the twelve participants originally identified as potential casualties just after training. National Training Laboratories (1969) also report some 33 participants out of 14,200 (less than 1 per cent) who may have been 'at risk' from their training. These later two studies are very weak ones indeed, but the one by Ross et al. provides some very important large scale support for low casualty rates from experiential learning groups.

Positive effects

Whether or not the figures quoted earlier of potential trainees 'at risk', both from our study and others, are acceptable or not, when making further training decisions, will depend to some extent on the potential payoffs or benefits these experiences offer. We have examined, therefore, the potentially positive effects of these groups as a method of social skill training for managers.

If we first examine the overall analysis of the data, we find that on balance these groups, *in toto*, in comparison to controls, show positive changes in trainees. In terms of personality changes experiential group participants in general become 'emotionally more stable' (higher ego strength), more 'trusting and adaptable', more 'humble and mild' but also more 'restrained and timid'. Although immediately after training (up to six weeks), they don't show any particularly significant positive change (nor negative) in either work or family relationships, after seven months they are seen by work colleagues as significantly improving their work 'relationships' and are seen by their friends and relatives as 'coping better with difficult family and personal problems'. It is interesting to note that at both six weeks and seven months after training they are still seen as having been 'emotionally affected' by the experience, although this drops slightly after seven months. Of the managers participating in experiential small group training 61 per cent are also seen *by at least two* of their fellow trainees as having shown positive change as a result of their experience, while 49 per cent are seen by at least one trainer as having changed in a positive direction. In terms of peer nominations of positive and negative effect there is considerable overlap; indeed, of the 77 participants named by at least one trainee as potentially 'hurt' by the group training programme, over two-thirds of them are also named by two or more trainees as having been 'helped'.

If we examine the data on an individual trainee basis (on corroborative information from two or more sources, e.g. family and work colleagues or other trainees and family, etc.), we find some very interesting results. Up to six weeks after training, some 35 participants (15 per cent of total trained population) are seen to have benefited significantly; 85 per cent of these are seen to show positive change in personality characteristics, 71 per cent are seen by their friends and relatives as improving their relationships, and 46 per cent are judged by work colleagues as benefiting from the training at work. If we take a very minimum requirement of at least one significantly positive change as seen by work colleagues or family or friends, then the number of improved participants rises to roughly 62 or 27 per cent.

If we follow up the original 35 participants after seven months, we find that 17 have internalised their learning and still show positive benefit, while 18 lapse into the 'no change' or very slight positive change category. None of these 18, however, could be classified as having experienced adverse effects at the follow-up period. In addition to the original 17, another 24 participants who were not identified as being particularly 'helped' at six weeks emerge as having benefited at seven months, making a total of 41 participants (18 per cent) showing positive gain in at least two aspects of their work and family life at the follow-up period (seven of these were previously designated as 'hurt' or 'at risk' at six weeks). If we include the participants who show marginal gains (on at least one criterion) the number rises to 54 (24 per cent). Most of these rigorously defined 'helped' (i.e. 41) participants show changes equally in both family and work life.

Comparison with previous studies

How do these results compare with the evaluation work already done on the positive effects of experiential group activities? A large number of studies (Cooper and Mangham, 1971) have been carried out evaluating the effects of small group training and they come up with roughly the same kind of conclusions. The earliest follow-up study was conducted by Miles (1965) and involved 34 American elementary school principals who had participated in two-week T-group laboratories. He used two control groups of untrained principals for comparison, one randomly chosen and the other nominated by the trainee principals. All were asked to describe, via an open-ended change-description questionnaire (similar to the one used in this study by work colleagues), the ways in which they had change their job-centred behaviour over an eight to ten months' period following the T-group. These self-reports were compared with similar descriptions completed by a number of their work associates: 73 per cent of the T-group trained participants, in comparison to 29 and 17 per cent of the nominated and random control groups respectively, were reported to have changed.

To test further the generality of Miles' findings, Bunker (1965) studied à sample of managers from six different training laboratories conducted by NTL. His basic methodology followed Miles in that he used a matched-pair control group obtained by participant nomination of work colleagues. Bunker used a total of 346 subjects, trained and controls. He found that 66.7 per cent of the T-group trained managers as compared to 33.3 per cent of controls were reported by their work associates to have positively changed. As with the Miles' study non-trained subjects were also perceived to have changed. A later study by Valiquet (1968) supported Bunker's results with 60 participants from T-group type programmes run *within* a company for its managers. He found roughly the same results as Miles and Bunker, that nearly two-thirds show positive change but that controls also show some change.

The only British study (Moscow, 1971) to use work colleagues' perception of change and which replicates the above studies, has shown that T-group participants drawn from management show changes very similar in type and frequency to those reported by Miles, Bunker and Valiquet.

And, finally, Boyd and Ellis (1962) made a further contribution by comparing the effects of a more conventional programme of human relations training built around case discussion and lectures. Both forms of training lasted for two weeks and were part of an in-company training programme for a Canadian utility company. There were 42 subjects, in three different groups, participating in the T-group training programme: 10 subjects in the lecture/case discussion programme, and 12 untrained nominated controls. The evaluation was made six weeks and six months after completion of the course and was assessed by interviewing work colleagues about behaviour at work; 36 per cent of the work colleagues of the non-trained control managers reported positive change for them, while 52 per cent did so for the lecture/case discussion participants and 70 per cent for the T-group trained participants.

In all these studies it was found that approximately 65-70 per cent of the participants show positive change as a result of experiential group training. This is at variance with the author's study, where, examining the data optimistically, we find between 20-30 per cent 'benefit or growth' rate. There are several reasons for this, however, First, our results are based on an individual analysis of the data in respect to the total trained and control samples. The participants identified as having 'benefited', therefore, were those who were significantly different (or approaching significance) from controls and the overall normative data for the trained groups. If we deduct from the 65-70 per cent of participants, the 30-35 per cent of untrained controls who seem to show 'natural change', [2] then we are very much closer to the figure we have obtained in this study. Nevertheless, using this calculation, the studies just reviewed are likely to have marginally larger numbers of 'benefited' participants because their determination of change is based on one criterion measure only, work colleagues' report of change, whereas the present study was based on a number of dependent variables requiring some degree of verified change from two or more sources.

Indeed, if we were to take just one source of data in this study, peer nominations of participants 'helped' by their training experience, and used the Bunker methodology of two or more positive reports irrespective of controls, we would find that 61 per cent of our participants (in this study) were named as having been 'helped' by the training.

Whether an optimistic rate of 25 per cent of participants showing positive or growth change as a result of experiential training is acceptable or not, cannot be fully answered here. One thing we can do, however, is point to the fact that this rate might be higher if this sort of training was 'in-company oriented'. Indeed one of the most impactful criticisms directed against this approach to social skill training for managers was levelled by Campbell and Dunnette (1968) in their comprehensive review of the effect of T-groups when they concluded 'while T-group training seems to produce observable change in behaviour, the utility of these changes for the performance of individuals in their organisational roles remains to be demonstrated'. Although most experiential groups are run on a 'stranger basis' (managers sent by different companies on a 'cultural island' type course), an increasing number are now organised within organisations and the results from the most recent studies examining the fade-out effect of learning from these latter programmes suggest they are more durable. Smith (1975) in his most recent survey of the field summarises his review by saying 'the highest rate of follow-up change is found among organisational groups who meet for training and remain intact thereafter'. 'Having discovered their ability to achieve certain goals within the sensitivity training setting, they are more likely to be able to continue doing so in their habitual settings'.

Experiential training conditions that create stress for managers

One of the main objectives of the research study was not only to assess the extent of disturbance which experiential groups may create, but also to try to identify the process or antecedent conditions that may help to contribute to distress or growth. There are a number of very interesting conclusions we can reach on the basis of the analysis.

First, that high risk group experiences, in the short term, are likely to be ones in which participants have desurgent (taciturn and sober) and threat-sensitive (shy and timid) personality predispositions, in a group which focuses on here-and-now social interaction and with trainers who are 'active energisers' (i.e. assertive, venturesome, and surgent or impulsive) but at the same time are 'open'. In addition, there is a tendency for the group experience itself to be slightly confronting, tense, intimate, person-centred, and unstructured, but with some

109

element of mutual support and trust.

Second, one of the best predictors of potential short term damage (up to six weeks after training) is the trainer personality/style and participant personality factors, as distinct from the group process variables or conditions of participation (e.g. reasons for attendance). In particular trainer personality attributes and styles of intervention seem the most potent aspect of potential risk in experiential learning groups for managers, which is consistent with the findings of Lieberman, et al. In their study they found that an 'aggressive stimulator' style of group leadership produced seven of the 16 casualties and they represented not only the most casualties but the most severe ones. These leaders or trainers were characterised by high stimulus input, intrusive, confronting and challenging behaviour but demonstrating some openness and positive regard. They were in essence the most charismatic but were also authoritarian.

In the present study, we found the trainers associated with the participants who were identified as being under short term psychological distress as a result of training, to be 'active energisers', that is, assertive, venturesome, surgent or impulsive but with some element of tendermindedness and openness. There is, therefore, a great deal of similarity between Lieberman et al.'s study and the author's, but it must be kept in mind that the above conclusion about trainer behaviour in this study was based on participants judged to be 'at risk' six weeks after training, the majority of whom show improvements and growth at a seven month follow-up period. Therefore, these trainer behaviour and personality characteristics may reflect desirable rather than undesirable attributes of group leader behaviour, which is the opposite point of view one would draw from the Lieberman et al. conclusions. In this context it is interesting to note the most recent review of group leader studies by Bolman (1976); in it he assessed all the empirical studies carried out on trainer behaviour and learning effectiveness, suggesting the following:

> The research suggests that the composite picture of the effective group leader includes the following characteristics: (1) The leader is able to empathize with the participants, and communicates a consistent respect and caring for them; (2) The leader is sufficiently congruent and genuine that participants experience him as trustable; (3) The leader is willing to be open, to confront, and to provide feedback, but does not do it in a way which is punishing

or which results in his completely dominating the group's activities.

It can be seen from Bolman's description that his effective group leader has qualities which Lieberman et al. might consider as potentially damaging (e.g. confronting, feedback, etc.). It is, therefore, *the degree and context of this type of trainer behaviour which may be responsible for either psychological growth or damage.* A confronting, assertive trainer with certain types of participants under certain group conditions has the potential for both enhancing or inhibiting the learning process.

Another interesting null result in our study was that short term distress was not associated with trainers who were emotionally unstable or anxiety-prone. This is contrary to many views (e.g. Mann, 1970) that some experiential group trainers are involved in this form of training to meet their own neurotic needs. None of the anxiety-related 16PF factors seems to be associated with groups or participants 'at risk'. Indeed, if we compare all the experiential group trainers in our study against the normative population data of the 16PF, we find that they are different from the norm on eight of the 12 scales (E, I, L; O, Q1, Q2, Q3 and Q4), and in a consistently positive direction. Experiential group trainers and facilitators are more tender-minded, more experimenting, more self-sufficient, more assertive, less suspicious, less apprehensive, less controlled, and less tense than the norm. So even if we were to find certain negative trainer personality traits associated with short term stress, this may indicate only marginally negative or disruptive trainer behaviour.

In addition to trainer personality and style of intervention, participant personality predispositions seem to be related to potential damage due to experiential training groups. If we examine all participants who have been nominated by fellow trainees as having been 'hurt' by the experience, we find that they tend to have personality characteristics associated with 'assertiveness' and 'tough-mindedness', that is, dominance or extraversion traits. If we extend our examination to participants more likely to have been damaged, that is, those identified as potentially 'at risk' on the basis of two or more criteria measures (e.g. family/ friends, work colleagues, etc.), and not just peer nominations, we find a very different set of participant characteristics linked to short term adverse effect. In this case, we find participants with introverted traits such as 'shy and timid', 'sober and taciturn', and 'more reserved' identified as individuals most 'at risk'. This apparent discrepancy in

111

results provides very interesting conceptual 'food for thought' about the kind of manager who may find experiential learning groups threatening.

The 'extroverted' executive is the one most likely to attract a great deal of *personal feedback* from others during training and it is only natural that other participants may, at the conclusion of the experience, feel that he may have suffered the most. The introvert rarely attracts much feedback, but when he does, he may find it has greater impact on him. The extrovert is likely to cope with negative feedback by rationalising, confronting, disconfirming information, while introverts may find dissonant information less easy to deal with, although their style or behaviour in groups (e.g. withdrawn) might not reveal this. A shy introverted, participant may find it very difficult to be a 'passive observer' in a group whose primary purpose is to focus on interpersonal behaviour and group dynamics, particularly in a group with a trainer who is assertive and impulsive. Nevertheless, it is these very people who may also benefit most from the experience, if the learning dynamics are carefully balanced to allow for the natural frailties of this type of personality.

It is very interesting to note that there was no evidence from the study that the executives who were identified as suffering short term distress as a result of training were less emotionally stable or anxious than other trainees. It has been suggested by Lakin (1969) and others (Crawshaw, 1969) that these types of group experiences attract people who are seeking and in need of therapy, i.e. individuals who are vulnerable, unstable and capable of being damaged. When we compared our managers with the normative population data on the 16PF, we found few differences between them (participants were more 'self-sufficient' and marginally more 'assertive'), and no differences on any of the anxiety-related factors.

Another aspect of the learning climate that may contribute to adverse effects from group training is the underlying philosophical approach and orientation of the programme. There is some evidence from this study, although not very strong (due to lack of opportunity to observe all training programmes), that groups with certain characteristics, whether preplanned or emergent, may create the conditions for short term (immediate post experience reactions) psychological distress. These are groups with a low amount of structure, high degree of confrontation, high level of intimacy, person- as distinct from group-centredness, and some 'tension' (but with some degree of mutual support and trust). Gottschalk and Pattison are among the few who have attempted to list the conditions causing what they call 'dramatic reactions' in groups. Among these are excessive expression of emotions, unstructuredness or situational ambiguity, group pressure to be 'open and intimate' and confrontation. House (1967) agrees with the above suggestion that experiential training can be dangerous for managers, in part because of 'pathologically *high affect* levels generated during the group sessions'. In the short run, our results are consistent with the thinking of House, Gottschalk and others. However, our data indicate that short term psychological distress may lead to long term benefit for a majority of participants identified as 'high risk' trainees.

This finding supports the view of Campbell and Dunnette (1968) that in the course of the development of a particular experiential learning group, factors such as the unstructured nature of the group process, emergence of here-and-now interaction norms, confrontation between participants, high degree of intimacy, etc., raise participants' anxiety levels, which in turn may serve as a catalyst for change, that is, they 'unfreeze' participants' behavioural repertoires. In a recent study by Rohrbaugh (1975) he has suggested 'existing (experiential) theory holds that enhancement of anxiety sets the stage for new learning by 'unfreezing' (cutting loose) participants from their usual ways of interacting, thus making it possible for feedback to have its maximum effect. Eventually, as participants try out new, more adaptive behaviour, new learning is reinforced by anxiety reduction'. He found that (a) anxiety was highest at the stage of experiential group development where unfreezing presumably occurred and (b) participants who appeared to learn most from the group experience also exhibited the sharpest decrease in arousal through the course of the training week.

These results seem consistent with our own information that the training programmes which had a large number of participants 'at risk', and were, therefore, high emotion arousal groups, were observed to show a decline in anxiety-stimulating behaviour over time. More detailed analysis would have to be done to confirm this adequately but this would certainly explain the improvement rate on managers formerly identified as 'at risk' after six weeks of training.

Another factor in the 'risk equation' is the conditions of participation of trainees. It was suggested earlier that one of the possible variables contributing to adverse effects of experiential groups could be associated with the participants' reasons for attending the training. Managers who are forced to attend by their organisations without any consultation or 'right of reply', it is argued, may be more vulnerable since they haven't self-selected themselves for the training. Certainly there is some evidence available (Cooper, 1975) although not conclusive, that psychometrically different participants may gravitate towards some programmes and not others. From our study, we were unable to find any relationship between a trainee's conditions of participation (whether organisationally forced to attend or self-selected by the trainee himself) and short term psychological distress or benefit. The reason for this may be that for a number of years now there has been concern expressed, in the training community at large, about the possible psychologically disruptive effects of these groups, which, ironically, may have led personnel and training officers to be more careful in the selection of potential trainees. The implication here is that although a number of managers are forced or by some subtle process encouraged to attend some of these experiences, the people responsible for assessing training needs and organising training opportunities have been either consciously or unconsciously screening the people they send. Awareness of the potential negative consequences of these experiences may have led them to avoid sending the more vulnerable managers, whereas in the early days of this training this may not have been the case.

Experiential training conditions that improve the social and interpersonal skills of managers

The process or learning variables associated with negative outcome participants were more easily identifiable than those for positive outcome participants. In addition, it was easier to draw conclusions from the data about participants identified as 'helped' in the short term (up to six weeks) than it was about participants judged at seven months. Nevertheless, there are a number of generalisations one might draw about effective group processes in the short term.

First, in most cases, participants who show some benefit from training have been in groups with trainers who were very supportive (both personally and at the group level), with a tendency to be somewhat relaxed and with low anxiety levels. In addition, these participants tend to have slightly 'apprehensive and tense' but 'conservative, controlled and self-sufficient' personality profiles. And, most importantly, there is a tendency to find them in groups which are less here-and-now oriented, with low levels of confrontation, little intimacy between participants and/or trainers, and with a more structured learning experience.

114

The personality and intervention style of trainers associated with managers who show some positive outcomes are not the dynamic 'energisers' they were for the short term casualty participants. They have a much less obvious profile, something like the 'social engineers' of the Lieberman et al. study. One might conclude, therefore, that, in the short run, managers who are identified as having 'benefited' from small group training find themselves in learning situations in which there is a 'socially supportive, low energiser' type of trainer, in a low emotional arousal type of group setting (little confrontation, intimacy, etc.), and are themselves individuals who are 'controlled but apprehensive' in social relationships. These participants are developing social skills in a context that is less threatening and perhaps more acceptable, in view of their own personality predispositions and needs.

If we examine these participants seven months after training we find that less than half of them have internalised the learning, and that a larger number of participants reappear as having 'benefited' from training, who were not so identified in the short term (indeed some of them were judged as having been 'at risk'). The identification (and inclusion) of an additional 24 participants (at the seven month follow-up period) as showing long term positive change, might explain why we find no clear cut differentiation in terms of training variables between the total number of participants judged as 'helped' and those not so judged at the later follow-up period. This is probably due to the fact that these participants are comprised of some who have been in an 'emotionally arousing' group and in the short term were distressed but in the long run have 'grown', some participants who have had a less dynamic and less emotionally arousing experience but one which was consistent with their own needs and learning strategy, and others who may have been in groups with elements of emotionality and structured social interaction. This fits in with Kiesler's (1973) theory of emotion. That is, that some people learn through a process of emotional arousal but only up to a certain point (and beyond that arousal detracts from it), and others through a more structured, low arousal process where they can affix behavioural labels to the phenomena being experienced. Therefore, participants with a learning style appropriate for the latter kind of group experience, who find themselves in dynamic, high arousal groups, may show no change (at the very least) and personal distress at the worst.

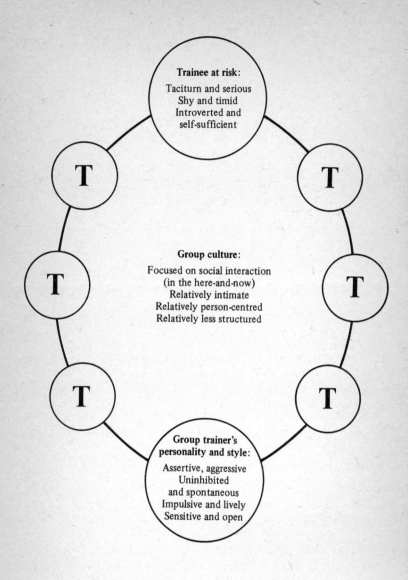

Fig. 6.1 Group processes in short term adverse experiences

Summary of experiential training conditions that impede and improve managerial relationships

Taking a look at the data of participants identified as having had some psychological distress and those having 'benefited' from training, we are able to draw a crude diagrammatical picture of the antecedent conditions which may be responsible for adverse effects as a result of experiential small groups.

It must be kept in mind that although Figure 6.1 summarises the likely group processes that may contribute to adverse effect from small group learning, a number of the participants experiencing these very dynamics and showing short term distress are seen in the longer term as having benefited. Thus, to some extent, these processes create the conditions for both psychological success and failure — the line between them is thin and the balance of trained predispositions, trainer needs, and group culture is tenuously drawn. Since only a small number of trainees who show long term change emerges from these types of learning conditions, the long term training gains and payoff may not be worth the risk.

By far the largest number of participants who showed benefit from training came from the following type of learning experience, as illustrated in Figure 6.2. While Figure 6.2 highlights the main process variables likely to lead to successful gain for participants in experiential groups in the short term, it leaves something to be desired in terms of a complete explanation in the long term. By far the largest group of participants who show follow-up growth from training emerge from the climate illustrated above. Some long term 'gain' participants (a small number admittedly), however, come from a learning environment diametrically opposed to the above (i.e. high emotionally arousing group). The former type of group process is a low risk and potentially high gain experience in both the short and long term for a broader group of participants, while the latter is a high risk and potentially distressful expereince in the short run and high gain experience for a more restricted group of participants in the long run.

The participants in the high risk type groups may not have gained much in the low risk groups and vice versa. We can never know for sure, but we may be able to plan more carefully for the maximum benefit for trainees by improving the manager/learning environment fit.

117

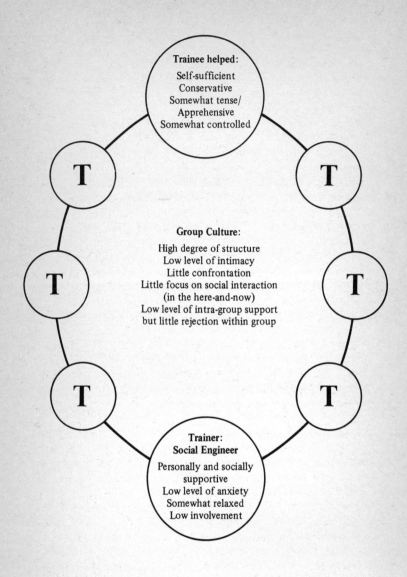

Trainee helped:

Self-sufficient
Conservative
Somewhat tense/
Apprehensive
Somewhat controlled

Group Culture:

High degree of structure
Low level of intimacy
Little confrontation
Little focus on social interaction
(in the here-and-now)
Low level of intra-group support
but little rejection within group

Trainer:
Social Engineer

Personally and socially
supportive
Low level of anxiety
Somewhat relaxed
Low involvement

Fig. 6.2   Group processes contributing to positive outcome

Implications

This research raises a number of practical training issues about experiential small groups as a method or ideology of social skill training for managers. The following are some of the questions raised not only by this research, but also by training and personnel officers and others who have to make decisions regarding managerial training in the human relations area.

First, should we send people on this form of training in view of its potential risk? Second, if we accept the potential benefit of this participative approach to social skill development, should we attempt to minimise the risk factor by: (1) screening out certain participants, (2) screening and/or training groups leaders, (3) screening out certain types of approaches to experiential group training? We will attempt to discuss the issues raised by each of these questions in the rest of the chapter. First, should those involved in management training continue to send people on these types of programmes? Looking both at the quantitative and qualitative data available to us in our investigation, it seems that the risk factor in experiential group training is quite low, particularly in the long term. Adding a margin of error, it seems to us that long term significant negative effects are unlikely to exceed 2-3 per cent of participants. It has been suggested that this sort of rate is no higher than the proportion of distressed people one might find in the population at large. Ross et al. (1971) summarise the concern of psychiatrists: 'major psychiatric reactions to participation in sensitivity training groups are not frequent or long-lasting and, in the opinion of psychiatrists whom we have surveyed, such adverse reactions are outweighed by beneficial influences'.

Although the above casualty rate is consistent with some other findings (Batchelder and Hardy, 1968; Ross et al. 1971) for different groups of trainees, one must be very careful indeed in trying to generalise these results to all experiential groups with all types of participants. In fact, a major *caveat* of the study is that we were assessing positive and adverse effect of groups among a well-established highly professional body of trainers, who over the years are likely to have gained the confidence of industry since they have attracted increasingly large numbers of trainees. Had we examined some of the more 'marginal' training and consultancy organisations, our results may have been very different indeed.

If we examine the overall data on our programmes as a whole, the trainers in our sample were slightly more psychometrically healthy, on

119

a number of psychological traits, than the normative population and were also seen by their trainees, on balance, as relatively competent and professional. Nevertheless, this form of training, in the short term, had a significant negative impact on between 5-10 per cent of the trainees. Indeed, a number of these were seen to change in a positive direction in the longer term and others to have had a 'fade out' of adverse effect, but what might have happened if the trainers were less skilled, more neurotic, less able to cope with 'highly charged affect', is still open to question.

The fact that many of the short term distressed managers in this investigation did not manifest longer term adverse effects is probably a tribute to the skill of the group leaders involved, in using and being able to exploit 'emotional arousal' as a learning mechanism. Unskilled, less sensitive group trainers may have enhanced the probabilities of both short and long term distress — the implications of this for trainer development will be discussed later.

It might be added that based on the evidence of this study and our knowledge of the management training field generally, the problems associated with the existence of large numbers of incompetent and unskilled trainers may not be as great as in the 'human potential movement' as a whole. One can only hypothesise and draw from one's own experience, but it is felt that the 'process of natural selection' among management training and consultancy organisations is likely to have eliminated a substantial number of the ineffective and potentially dangerous trainers. However, where experiential groups are used in the wider community as 'personal growth experiences', this 'natural process' may have been less effective and the dangers greater. Whether this accurately or inaccurately reflects the 'state of the art' in human relations training should not make us complacent about the consequences of the behaviour of individual management trainers who may be involved in this kind of training without the requisite competence. We should seriously consider ways of developing these people further or finding ways to screen them out of such activities.

Another side of the question is 'of what benefit are those groups?' Are enough people changed in a significantly positive way to accept the potential risk? We found in our study, excluding changes related to the simple passage of time and everyday life, that about 20-25 per cent of the managers showed some significantly positive outcome. When making the necessary adjustments to the results of other studies, to make them comparable to our own, the benefit rate found here is slightly lower than the others, but this may be accounted for by the fact that we used corroborative criteria of success (e.g. from two or more sources).

It is very difficult for us here to dictate to others what might be an acceptable success rate for training, since to do this adequately we would have to know something about the success and risk rates for alternative methods of social skill training. Unfortunately, most other approaches to human relations training have not assessed the possible negative consequences of their programmes and very little positive outcome data are available on them as well. Campbell (1971) has highlighted this in his review, where he found that over 60 per cent of the empirical evaluation work in human relations training was in the area of experiential and sensitivity training. In addition, in the non-experiential or general human relations programmes, the only data available are in the form of group means, so that we are unable to arrive at even a rough estimate of the number of individual trainees 'positively changed' to make comparisons between training alternatives. One suspects that not many management training programmes produce meaningful and long lasting change in more than 30 per cent of their participants, if that. This may be due to the fact that much of this training is being done by organisations outside the context of the managers' actual work groups. In experiential management training, for example, it has been suggested by Pugh (1965) that one of the main reasons for this low, long lasting change rate may be due to the large numbers of managers sent on 'stranger groups' and not enough groups being run 'within' organisations. The issue here is quite straightforward: can individuals participating in experiential activities — composed of managers from different companies and held in 'cultural island' conditions — transfer their learning outcomes to their organisations as intended?

It is interesting to note that although 61 per cent of the participants in this study were seen by two or more other trainees as having been helped or changed positively as a result of training, in the final analysis only around 20-25 per cent were identified as showing long lasting positive effects. Indeed, research work was reported in the late 1960s which suggested that organisational training laboratories, composed of work groups or diagonal slices of managers at different levels within the organisation, might provide an opportunity for greater transfer of learning and more long lasting effects of training (Friendlander, 1967). These approaches to social skill training may, therefore, be more effective than the 'stranger' groups examined in this study, but we may

121

also be forced to examine the potentially negative consequences of them as well. It might be argued, however, that the positive-outcome-to-risk ratio is likely to be higher since transfer of learning may be greater and the necessity of working through issues with colleagues one sees every day may have a more 'dampening' effect on the level of emotionality (which has no comparable natural limits in 'stranger groups' in cultural island settings).

A number of psychiatrists also see limitations in 'stranger groups', as Gottschalk and Pattison (1969) emphasise: 'the T-group has often been conducted with little concern for how the learning in the T-group setting is to be transferred to the on-the-job setting. Trainers may assume that transfer of learning will occur automatically, that attending to transfer issues may interfere with the group process, or that the T-group experience is intrinsically valuable and the transfer of learning to the job or community is in a sense irrelevant'.

Although a more positive outcome might be achieved by utilising experiential groups *within* the organisation and work group, we are forced to proceed here from the position that 'stranger-type' group programmes are being run on the wider managerial community, that managers volunteer or are sent on such courses, and that these experiences, under certain conditions, may be having measurable negative consequences, particularly in the short run.

What we must next ask ourselves is what can we do to minimise this risk, and, hopefully, enhance their effectiveness? It has been suggested by many (Jaffe and Scherl, 1969; Gottschalk and Pattison, 1969; Mann, 1970) that the three most important areas for action are: in participant selection or screening, training and screening of group leaders, and screening of various approaches or orientations to experiential group training.

First, the selection and screening of participants. Jaffe and Scherl (1969) have proposed a number of suggestions to minimise the possibility of psychological disturbance of these groups:

1 That participation be completely and truly voluntary.
2 That participation be based on informed consent with respect to purpose and goals. Each person should know clearly ahead of time what will occur, over how long a time, for what purposes, with what degree of confidentiality, and with what specific potential dangers. Participants should be warned that these groups are not intended for therapy nor are they intended for persons who con-

sider themselves or fear they are 'sick' or in 'need of treatment'.

3 That participants be screened at least by questionnaire and preferably by interview.

4 That participants understand what types of behaviour are permissable during the group.

5 That follow-up for all participants be available to help deal with group termination.

Second, another major concern about experiential groups has to do with the trainers or group leaders. Yalom and Lieberman (1971) suggest that one of the major findings in their study is that the number and severity of casualties are almost a direct result of a particular leadership style, indeed, they say 'the casualties seemed truly *caused* not merely hastened or facilitated, by the leader style, and is thereby preventable by a change in leader style'. They found that adverse effects were created by group leaders characterised by intrusive, aggressive, and confronting behaviour.

We found a not too dissimilar pattern of characteristics associated with trainers in our groups, who may have helped to create the conditions for short term distress. But in our case the long term effects of this leadership were minimal; indeed, the impact of high energiser-type trainers may have provided an impetus to long term positive change for *some* of the participants. The *caveat* here, however, is that an aggressive, confronting, high energising leadership style in trainers with less experience and who are less well-adjusted then the ones taking part in this study may have created an unacceptably high number of long term casualties. In our view one should consider very carefully the skills that experiential group leaders should possess. Many of the group trainers currently involved in this form of training, both in management education and elsewhere in the UK, possess some minimal level of insight into group and individual phenomena, obviously some more than others. But there are two skills many of these trainees could be encouraged to acquire, in an effort to minimise potentially negative effects and indeed to enhance the possibility of greater success in their groups. Ross et al. have suggested one of these, albeit a bit too extreme, since Ross writes from the viewpoint of a psychiatric clinician:

the training of the group leader in some clinical setting becomes mandatory if he is to perceive subtle reactions of disorganization before they become full-blown. In addition, he should have suf-

ficient clinical experience to be beyond the use of affective dis-
charge and catharsis for its sake alone . . . . The leader must be
alert to step in and protect members of the group from promis-
cuous attack.

In part we would concur with this recommendation, particularly that
experiential group leaders, even in the field of management education,
should attempt to obtain some training in being able to recognise and
cope with participants 'at risk'. This would ensure not only a lower
level of casualty but also that the group leader has the skills to deal
with it when it occurs. At the moment no such training programme is
available in the UK or the US.

Another important aspect has to do with the group trainer's understanding of his own behaviour and how this might lead to adverse or
success effects. Each group leader behaves in a way, as we have seen in
this study, that creates conditions for both psychological success and
failure, which is related in no small measure to his own needs and
psychological make-up (Argyris, 1967). The trainer can exploit his role
in the pursuance of his own needs, particularly in his desire to be liked
or to exercise power. To reiterate Schein and Bennis' (1965) message
'the possibilities for unconscious gratification in the trainer's role are
enormous and because of their consequence (for the health of the
client as well as the trainer) they must be examined'. It is essential
that training programmes be developed that focus on the trainer's
motives and how these may enable, or prevent, the manager from
learning in his own way.

In addition to trainer development programmes, it is important that
group leaders in these types of learning experiences have extensive
group experience prior to 'solo training', where they can receive feedback, try out different behavioural styles and approaches, and generally
learn to cope with the variety of phenomena that takes place in different groups with different populations and compositions. In Britain
at the moment there are very few opportunities for the *comprehensive*
training of group leaders, whereas in Holland, the US and Australia
there are well designed, thoroughly conceived programmes which at
the very least are likely to be providing fewer unskilled and potentially
disruptive management trainers.

The last question we would like to focus on is 'are certain types or
approaches to group training potentially more damaging or less beneficial than others?' On balance, we found in our study, examining both

the positive and negative outcome participants and groups together, that the most supportive, structured, and least confronting (e.g. intimate, challenging, etc.) experiences are likely to produce the most benefit with the least risk, although there is also information available which suggests that the opposite of these conditions can also prove beneficial in the long run for a limited number of managers. In terms of structure, this fits in with the findings of Ross et al. on the relationship between lack of structure and the likelihood of acute trainees disorganisation. They found only five cases of adverse reactions among 1,750 participants in managerial grid groups, and they concluded that 'the percentage of reactors (0.28 per cent) for these more structured, task-oriented groups is lower than the 0.66 per cent overall figure, including miscellaneous T-groups and sensitivity groups'. Bradford and Eoyang (1976) support in principle the view that structured exercise-based groups provide the psychological safety in which risk-taking can occur and be fruitfully used. They argue that this is particularly relevant when the individual is trying out new behaviour. In an unstructured group 'a person can feel very vulnerable being the only one trying a behaviour in which he does not feel very competent. Another constraint can be the fear that others might see that as 'being me' (so if I self-disclose some feelings of inadequacy, will others see me as a weak person?). If it is part of an exercise, then that behaviour is separated from being a personality attribute of the individual'. The point here is that many people may need structure to provide them with the security to learn, to risk-take, and to experiment. Learning environments which are too unstructured, too confronting, too intimate may disorient rather than facilitate change.

On balance, from our results and other work, structured experiences are likely to be safer and for a larger number of participants likely to produce more positive change, while unstructured ones may be slightly more risky but capable of producing the extent and quality of change found in structured groups, but probably with smaller numbers of participants. The current trend is unmistakably in the direction of more structured and less 'emotionally arousing' management training activities. Whether this is due to an implicit understanding of the potential risks involved or to some natural sociological phenomenon cannot be accurately determined, but it may lead to fewer expressed concerns about the dangers of experiential management training.

What may be more crucial, however, is not whether an experience is a structured or unstructured one but whether it creates the conditions under which the individual trainee's needs are met and his own learning strategy is allowed free expression. Argyris (1967) gets close to this when he suggested that the necessary learning conditions for psychological success in laboratory education were: (1) that the participant should define his own learning goal; (2) that he should develop the path to this goal; (3) that he should control the centrality of the needs involved and finally (4) that he should control the strength of the challenge. Many of the structured group experiences in our study provided the rough limits or boundaries to meet participants' security and safety needs, but they allowed participants a margin of flexibility in choosing their own learning opportunities. It may be this combination of factors and not simply the degree of *structure* of the experience which leads to positive change.

Most people concerned about group training recognise that some element of *support* in groups is a necessary precondition not only in minimising casualties but also in promoting growth. Gottschalk and Pattison (1969) have suggested that 'the T-group has often ignored the necessity and utility of ego defenses . . . . Often little attention is paid to the necessity for support and nurturance . . . . Some leaders have even theorized on the value of some type of total exposure. This ignores individual differences in the capacity to tolerate stress and frustration. The mode of the self-reliant man who can take anything the group dishes out, may more often be the covert norm than adjusting the group's expectations to the needs, capacities, and interests of each person'.

It is very difficult, if not impossible, to attempt to prescribe the kind of experiential group approach one should attend, since much of this depends on the needs and characteristics of the manager, the type of authority style he can cope with and learn from, and what his objectives or aims of attending the training are in the first instance.

We are in a much more difficult position *vis-à-vis* making recommendations about experiential groups than Lieberman et al. who were dealing with a much less stable population (Smith, 1975) than ours, but in their summation they exclaimed 'individuals who are psychologically vulnerable and who over-invest their hopes in the magic of salvation through encounter groups are particularly vulnerable when they interact with leaders who believe that they can offer deliverance. Such an interaction is a potent synergistic force for destructive outcome'. How can anyone disagree with this, but how does that help us in the field of management education? On balance, managers attending such exper-

126

iences are not neurotically seeking 'managerial salvation' but attempting to improve their social or human relations skills by a technique which is involving, interesting and seems to produce some positive change — or, at least, that is what managers are led to believe. Our best means of trying to minimise the potential risks of these types of experiences are two-fold; (a) more detailed *information* to prospective participants so that they may be able to self-select the most appropriate training approaches for themselves and avoid those approaches which may be incompatible with their needs and/or coping styles, and (b) to introduce some degree of control of the management trainers involved in this kind of learning experience.

Notes

1 Data were also collected on 96 control managers who were on waiting lists for one of the small group training programmes of a similar one used in this study.
2 This figure of natural change is possibly attributable (1) to real change occasioned by events other than experiential group activity, which have no monopoly of the change market and (2) to the fact that when respondents are asked to accommodate a researcher by providing change descriptions they may hate to disappoint him and so tend to look for something to put down. It is important to keep this base rate of change in mind, however, in eliminating 'positive changers'.

References

Argyris, C., 'On the future of laboratory education', *Journal of Applied Behavioral Science*, 1967, 3(2), pp. 153-83.
Batchelder, R.L., and Hardy, J. M., *Using Sensitivity Training and the Laboratory Method*, Associated Press, New York 1968.
Blanchard, W., 'Ecstasy without agony is baloney', *Pschology Today*, 1970, 3(8), 8.
Bolman, L. in Cooper, C.L., *Developing Social Skills in Managers*, Macmillan, London 1976, pp. 37-51.
Boyd, J.B., and Ellis, J.D., *Findings of Research into Senior Management Seminars*, Hydro-Electric, Toronto 1962.
Bradford, D., and Eoyang, C., in Cooper, C.L., *Developing Social Skills in Managers*, Macmillan, London, 1976, pp. 52-62.

Bunker, D.R., 'Individual Applications of Laboratory Training', *Journal of Applied Behavioral Science*, 1965, 1, pp. 131-48.

Campbell, J.P., 'Personnel training and development', *Annual Review of Psychology*, 1971, 22, pp. 565-602.

Campbell, J.P., and Dunnette, M.D., 'Effectiveness of T-group Experiences in Management Training and Development', *Psychological Bulletin*, 1968, 70, pp. 73-104.

Cooper, C.L., 'How psychologically dangerous are T-groups and encounter groups?' *Human Relations*, 1975, 28, (3), pp. 249-60.

Cooper, C.L., *Learning from Others in Groups*, Associated Business Press, London 1979.

Cooper, C.L., and Bowles, D., 'Physical encounter and self disclosure,' *Psychological Reports*, 1973, 33, pp. 451-5.

Cooper, C.L., and Mangham, I.L., *T-groups: a survey of research*, John Wiley and Sons, London 1971.

Crawshaw, R., 'How sensitive is sensitivity training?' *American Journal of Psychiatry*, 1969, 126, pp. 870-3.

Friedlander, F., 'The impact of organizational training laboratories upon the effectiveness and interaction of on-going work groups', *Personnel Psychology*, 1967, 20(3), pp. 289-309.

Gottschalk, L.A., and Pattison, E.M., 'Psychiatric perspective on T-groups, and the laboratory movement: an overview', *American Journal of Psychiatry*, 1969, 126, pp. 823-39.

House, R.J., 'T-group education and leadership effectiveness', *Personnel Psychology*, 1967, 20, pp. 1-32.

Jaffe, S.L., and Scherl, D.J., 'Acute psychosis precipitated by T-group experiences', *Archives of General Psychiatry*, 1969, 21, pp. 443-8.

Kiesler, S., 'Emotion in groups', *Journal of Humanistic Psychology*, 1973, 13, (3) pp. 19-31.

Lakin, M., 'Some ethical issues in sensitivity training', *American Psychologist*, 1969, 24, pp. 923-8.

Lieberman, M.A., Yalom, I.D., and Miles, M.B., *Encounter Groups: First Facts*, Basic Books, New York 1973.

Mann, E.K., 'Sensitivity training: should we use it?' *Training Development Journal*, 1970, 24, pp. 44-8.

Miles, M.B., 'Changes during and following laboratory training', *Journal of Applied Behavioral Science*, 1965, 1, (3), pp. 215-43.

Moscow, D., 'T-group training in the Netherlands: an evaluation and cross-cultural comparison, *Journal of Applied Behavioral Science*, 1971, 7, pp. 427-48.

National Training Laboratory, News and Reports, 1969, 3, 4.

Pugh, D., T-group training from the point of view of organization theory', in Whitaker, G., *T-group Training*, Blackwell, Oxford, 1965, pp. 44-50.

Rohrbaugh, M., 'Patterns and correlates of emotional arousal in laboratory training', *Journal of Applied Behavioral Science*, 1975, 11, (2), pp. 220-40.

Ross, W.D., Kligfeld, M., and Whitman, R.W., 'Psychiatrists, Patients and Sensitivity Groups', *Archives of General Psychiatry*, 1971, 25, pp. 178-80.

Schein, E.H., and Bennis, W.G., *Personal and Organizational Change Through Group Methods*, Wiley, 1965.

Smith, P.B., 'Are there adverse effects of sensitivity training?' *Journal of Humanistic Psychology*, 1975, 15, (2), pp. 29-47.

Valiquet, M.I., 'Individual change in a management development program', *Journal of Applied Behavioral Science,* 1968, 4, pp. 313-25.

Yalom, I.D., and Lieberman, M.A., 'A study of encounter group casualties', *Archives of General Psychiatry,* 1971, 25, pp. 16-30.